AF270165

QREATIVE EVOLUTION

QREATIVE EVOLUTION

How to Question Everything to Find Your Creative Fulfillment

Louis Henry Mitchell

Creative Director, Sesame Workshop

BLACK STONE PUBLISHING

Printed in the United States of America

First edition: 2025
ISBN 979-8-212-40983-4
Self-Help / Creativity

Version 1

Blackstone Publishing
31 Mistletoe Rd.
Ashland, OR 97520

www.BlackstonePublishing.com

To my dear, beloved mother, Justa C. Mitchell,
who loved me, believed in me, and encouraged me above
and beyond all of the naysayers, and to Charlotte Landau,
the greatest art teacher of my entire life. Each woman
taught me that the only true work of art is life itself.

**Everyone is an artist.
We create our lives,
moment by moment,
decision by decision.
See your life as your work of art,
living your life with purpose,
rather than by chance.**
—Louis Henry Mitchell

TABLE OF CONTENTS

INTRODUCTION

You are creative. All humans are. Creativity is an endowment bestowed upon each of us at birth.

You may have picked up *Qreative Evolution* in hopes of expanding your creative gifts. Or you may struggle to believe that you are particularly creative. Perhaps you are interested in learning how to use your creative powers to infuse your life with joy. Maybe you want to know how to live in a more creative way or access your innate creativity more easily. You may be curious about the connection between creativity and problem-solving, productivity, personal happiness, tolerance and a number of other powerful, life-affirming qualities. Or there may be another reason—or reasons—you'd like to immerse yourself in a creative lifestyle.

My name is Louis Henry Mitchell. As an artist, creativity educator, and creative director of character design at Sesame Workshop, creativity has fueled not only my career but my life. You'll learn about my own creative education from *Qreative Evolution*, which was born from the experiences I've had as I've lived life, overcome obstacles, and reached for my dreams. For years, I have shared what I've learned in a series of educational workshops, presentations, and talks on creativity. For now, however, I want to offer you a preview of what you'll discover in the pages ahead.

Let's start at the beginning, with the word "creativity." To paraphrase the *Encyclopedia Britannica*, "Creativity is the ability to make or otherwise bring into existence something new, whether a new solution to a problem, a new method or device, or a new artistic object or form." Just as each human being is unique, so is each human being's creativity. Some people are gifted cake decorators, gift wrappers, oil painters, computer programmers, architects, composers, fashion designers, recipe developers, cartoonists, or some other wonderful thing. I hope you see where I am going with this: Creativity is not limited to one type of creation. Please remember this whenever you feel tempted to compare yourself to someone else. You already are an artist. You are creating your life every single moment, whether you realize it or not.

But before I tell you more about what you'll discover in this book, I want to share just a bit about my own creative journey. What you are about to read proves that creativity is the result of participating in your own life—in a way that honors who you are and what you love.

When I was a young boy living with my mother in Brooklyn, New York, I was obsessed with drawing, comic books, animation, and puppets. In hindsight, visual art was my personal type of creativity, but at the time I had no idea my love of these things would lead me onto a creative path that would, in turn, lead me to people and places I had only dreamed of. One of these places was, literally, *Sesame Street*.

I watched *Sesame Street* throughout my childhood. Even as a young boy, I appreciated how the show helped educate children about humanity and kindness, as well as how it represented individuals of different races and abilities, allowing all of us to see ourselves as an important part of a beautiful world. I was especially fascinated with *Sesame Street*'s puppets, called Muppets. Whenever a Muppet came on screen, time stood still as I focused on the character. Through a series of creative events—which didn't seem related at the time—I would grow up to become the creative director of character design for *Sesame Street*. This was beyond a miracle to me. I realized that my creativity is what led me toward a career at *Sesame Street*. Simply put, my childhood enthusiasm for art helped me evolve into an artist suited to drawing *Sesame Street* Muppets. As I considered my good fortune, I realized that creativity is a conduit for good things. It is the manifestation of opportunities that move you toward your best life—if you are willing to nurture your creative gifts.

As you read *Qreative Evolution*, I want two things: for you to discover your creative gifts, and for you to use these gifts to create the life you are meant to live.

Throughout *Qreative Evolution*, I share the self-evolution path that is available to any individual willing to nurture his or her creativity. Engage in your own form of creativity and the path will be revealed. As you interact with your talent and invest time, energy, and thought into your creativity, you evolve. You receive clarity. You discover your purpose. You realize how you are meant to spend your time, and how you are meant to live your life. For me, this evolution meant following my love of art down a path that included drawing, Muppets, and creativity education. For you, self-discovery will be a path filled with something uniquely your own and equally wonderful.

Creativity is life's gift to you. Creativity's purpose is to delight you as you enjoy it for yourself, and as you share it in service to others. Creativity is energy. It is possibility. It is one of our most powerful human qualities, responsible for everything from da Vinci's *Mona Lisa* to Beethoven's Symphony No. 9, hip-hop to indoor plumbing, the Taj Mahal to your neighborhood playground. Put another way, creativity is behind every creation in our lives. It is also responsible for letting us be more human, more powerful, more attentive, more joy-filled, more helpful, more industrious, more curious, more accepting, and more in love with life and all the possibilities life holds.

If you are unsure what those creativity possibilities might be for you, let me reassure you, whenever I state that everyone is an artist, I usually get the following questions in return:

"Are you sure that everyone is an artist? I feel as if I'm the most uncreative person alive."

"Can I really learn how to be more creative?"

"I am not artistic. Is there another way I can be creative?"

"How can I harness creativity to get ahead at work?"

"Will creativity make me smarter (or happier or healthier or more attractive)?"

"Can I use creativity to strengthen the quality of my relationships?"

"Is nurturing my creativity difficult?"

"Does nurturing my creativity take a lot of time?"

"Will my life expand as my creativity expands?"

I wrote *Qreative Evolution* to answer these and many other questions you may have about being creative. As you move through the book, you'll come across what I call "trusts." Note that I chose the word "trust," as in a precious commodity en-*trust*ed to us, to use for the good of ourselves and others. The guidance these trusts provide will support you as you grow. They consist of stories, examples, exercises, lifestyle enhancements, positive habits, and mindset shifts which you can use to find, expand, nurture, and make use of your own personal creativity.

To illustrate how these trusts can help you, I open each chapter with a personal story that portrays how I discovered a specific trust. The chapter headings have powerful and unusual names because I want to emphasize the theme of each one as an anchor; a way to remember the key points given in each chapter. Throughout the book, I share lessons, challenges, triumphs, personal research, and, of course, fun creativity-building assignments to help you understand and integrate what you've read.

We live in a time of unprecedented distraction, making it easy to hand off our creativity to search engines, smartphones, Siri, artificial intelligence, and more. This is a mistake that robs us of one of the most glorious things about being human: our innate creativity.

The world needs your creativity to help solve problems and design solutions for the challenges humankind faces. In return, we—the individuals who inhabit this world—need each other's creativity to reach our fullest potential, to delight and energize us, and to create the human connections that help us thrive.

As you cultivate your creativity—and increasingly enjoy the many gifts that come with using it—you will inevitably bump up against obstacles. I call these "assignments," because in truth, anything that highlights *what is not working* is a lesson. The snags you face are opportunities, which encourage you to search outside of the proverbial box for answers. I mention this because I want to assure you that an obstacle can act as a launch-pad to help you grow your creative life.

Your own creativity is the purpose of *Qreative Evolution.* In these pages, you'll discover best creative practices, guidance to help you move forward, advice to help you face whatever (or whomever) challenges you, plus fresh ways to see and use your creativity.

Finally, for those of you who want to explore your creativity more deeply, I've included an extensive collection of resources to enjoy.

I am eager to share *Qreative Evolution* with you. May you embrace your creative journey through our adventure here to-gether.

Thank you for taking this journey with me.

Gratefully,

Louis Henry Mitchell

Chapter One

QREATIVE EVOLUTION

Qreative Evolution is a guide that's meant to accompany you as you discover your innate creativity. We begin our journey with personal stories. Stories often contain lessons, and sometimes we don't see those lessons until we tell our stories, allowing us to see how everyday actions can help us grow. This is why I open each chapter of *Qreative Evolution* with a personal story that shares an experience from my own past, and the lessons I learned from that particular experience. However, I do need to preface these stories with one request: Please read with an open mind. I realize that acknowledging my achievements might be regarded as boasting, but it took me many years to learn that doing so shows not only an appreciation for what I have achieved but also gratitude for those who've supported me.

Sharing my path with you hopefully inspires you to discover the path to your own creativity. This has not been an easy road to travel, but I learned so much about appreciating the journey of life, even during some of the most difficult times of my life. It took me a very long time to understand that, just like the triumphs and victories of life, the hardships and challenges are also part of what can make us great if seen through the right perspective. Whenever people share stories about their successes, they celebrate humanity as a whole. Those who hear and read success stories realize that they, too, can succeed. With that, I can now share the first of many stories that led to my own personal *Qreative Evolution*.

SO, HOW DID I GET TO *SESAME STREET*?

I have always been deeply fascinated with puppets. As a child, the one place I was able to see puppets was on television. I enjoyed watching the little mouse puppet named Topo Gigio and, more than anything else, I loved the Muppets. One day, on *The Ed Sullivan Show*, I heard Mr. Sullivan say in his famous voice, "And now, here are the Muppets!"

I was six years old.

For so many weeks, every time I heard him say that I dropped what I was doing, ran into the living room, and slid in front of the television set. One day, after the Muppets performed, Ed Sullivan greeted a tall, bearded man who held a Muppet in one hand. Just then it dawned on me: *You mean a* man *was doing that?* Up until that moment, I wasn't aware that a human was responsible for bringing a Muppet "to life." I cannot explain what shifted within me in that moment, but I believe that realization changed my life's trajectory: If a man was making that puppet perform, maybe I could do that, too.

Colorful homemade puppets began appearing in my toy box, all bearing a significant resemblance to the socks that went missing from my sisters' drawers. *Sesame Street* hadn't yet been created, but that didn't matter. I was increasingly drawn, throughout my childhood and into my adulthood, to Jim Henson and his Muppets.

On November 10, 1969, *Sesame Street* debuted. In my mind, it was the show of all shows. As I studied *Sesame Street*'s characters, I realized that the show's puppets were all creations of the very same bearded man I saw talking to Ed Sullivan on TV: Jim Henson.

Throughout my life, I kept the hope of working for *Sesame Street* deep in my heart. I encountered much opposition to this dream, from many people. The most came from my father. He had left me, my mother, and my two older sisters when I was four years old, but he remained an occasional presence throughout my life. He didn't share much about his youth, but I did know he'd had a traumatic childhood. Born in Alabama in 1903, he was almost sixty years old when I was born. All he wanted for me was to join the army so I would always have free veteran's health benefits. I wanted more than that, however, even if I didn't know how to go about getting it. My father didn't want to hear about me becoming an artist. He would discourage me by telling me I wasn't going to make anything of it.

"The hardest challenge is to be yourself in a world where everyone is trying to make you somebody else."

—E. E. CUMMINGS

"Don't pay any attention to that," my mother would simply say. "Just keep going."

My precious mother was my champion who had overcome her own obstacles. She didn't put my father down or make a big deal of his—or anyone else's—discouragement. Her encouragement protected me from the voices that said, "You'll never make it."

Later, I attended college at the School of Visual Arts in New York City. During my second year there, a thought came to me: *Maybe my professor can help me achieve my dream of drawing for* Sesame Street. I often thought about what I would say to him. Even though I was doing well in school, it was some time before I was brave enough to approach my teacher. When I finally shared my aspirations with him, he interrupted me before I could get the words out of my mouth.

"Oh, Louis, you're *never* going to get a job there," the professor said. "I believe in you, but you're aiming *way* too high. You need to aim lower, toward goals you can achieve. But *Sesame Street*? You're never going to get that job."

I was crushed. When my mother got home that afternoon from her nursing job, she saw me looking like I had just lost my best friend.

"What's wrong with you?" she asked.

I told her what my teacher had said.

"Well, does he work at *Sesame Street*?"

"No."

Her voice rose slightly as she asked, "Then why are you listening to him? If they don't want you at *Sesame Street* let *them* tell you. But don't listen to somebody who doesn't even work there."

While this made perfect sense, the sting of my teacher's words was too fresh, and it took years before I was able to admit my dream to anyone out loud.

I had family and friends in the neighborhood who couldn't see a future for themselves, and they didn't see one for me, either.

"You know you're wasting your time with this art, right?" they'd often say. "You're never going to make it."

The first person other than my mom who encouraged me to see the possibility of being an artist was my eighth-grade art teacher, Mrs. Charlotte Landau. I talk more about her later on, but I want to say here that she was an artist herself with a nice husband and family, she taught art, and she had a house in the neighborhood. She showed me that a person could be a successful artist and still have a "normal" life.

> In your life, who was the first person outside of your family who encouraged you and showed you—by example—what success could look like for you? Who discouraged you and perhaps even shamed you for wanting to succeed at something you loved?

At age seventeen, while still in school, I began my career as a freelance illustrator. As the years passed, my career progressed. In my early thirties, I was working for various companies, doing everything from freelance art direction to full-time character design. I even freelanced a bit for the Jim Henson Company, which gave me hope that I could someday work full-time, on-staff for *Sesame Street.*

So, I put together a portfolio of Muppet drawings to show them how much more I could do as a staff artist. I worked incredibly hard on those drawings. I submitted and resubmitted this portfolio to the Jim Henson Company several times but always received the same response: "Your work is very good, but we don't have any work for you."

This went on for eight months.

Desperate for some type of positive response, I began sending my work to them weekly. One day, as I approached their offices, I thought about my former professor. Maybe he was right about me never getting a job with *Sesame Street.* As I replayed his words in my head, I grew discouraged. *How much longer can I do this?* I asked myself.

I had reached a point where I could no longer take the rejection, so I made a promise to myself: If *Sesame Street* didn't offer me some kind of work that day, I would quit submitting my drawings to them. I didn't have the heart to tell my mother or anyone else about my decision to give up. So, one last time I dropped off the portfolio, hoping it would get into the hands of someone who would give me a chance.

The subway ride home was torturous. Should nothing come of this last attempt, I knew I would make good on my private promise to give up. I didn't want to disappoint my mother after all the encouragement she had given me, but I just could not take it anymore.

When I got home, as nervous as I was, I looked over at the answering machine. There was a message on it. One of the art directors at the Jim Henson Company had left me a message: "Hello, Louis, this is Jim Mahon from Muppets. I just saw your portfolio and like what you're doing. I'd like you to come up to the office so I can get you started on a project."

I knew I wasn't dreaming because my heart was beating faster than it ever had. I returned Mr. Mahon's call and made an appointment for the next morning. He was wonderful to me. He assigned me to do an ink drawing of Ernie that was going to be a small decal on a pair of toddler sneakers. It took me six months before I could properly draw Big Bird, but by then, I was a regular freelance artist for Mr. Mahon. Twenty-four years had passed from the time I fell in love with the Muppets, to the time I sat down in my own office at Sesame Workshop, the nonprofit company that produces *Sesame Street*.

I had made it to *Sesame Street*.

When I called my father to tell him, he said five words I never thought I would hear from him: "I guess I was wrong." Growing up, I didn't get a whole lot from my father, but what I got that day made up for everything he never gave me.

My father's acceptance had a greater impact on my life than I could have realized. He never again discouraged my dreams of being an artist. Because she had always believed in me, my mother absolutely gloated, although she did make sure that I knew my success was the result of hard work, perseverance, and learning to believe in myself.

The lesson for me was to keep persevering. I have worked for *Sesame Street*—the show that has captured my imagination from childhood—since 1992. It all started with a small freelance job and has blossomed into opportunities even beyond my wildest dreams.

THE NAYSAYERS DON'T GET A VOTE

A naysayer is someone who says no to you about your goals and dreams. It could be a coworker who points out how unlikely it is that you'll be considered for a promotion, or a friend who hints at how "impossible" it is to write a book or start a business. A naysayer might be a family member who doesn't believe you have the ability to achieve something different than what you have now.

People shoot down each other's desires and discourage their growth for different reasons. Some are threatened by another's advancement—dragging a dreamer down is easier than joining them as they reach for their goals. Others are pessimists and feel that nothing ever changes, so why bother? Others may come from a place of genuine—and misguided—concern. My father, for example, thought that by discouraging my artistic career, he could steer me toward something that (in his limited experience) seemed more stable.

Regardless of the naysayers in your life, remember that you came into this life with creative gifts. Nurture these creative gifts by refusing to give the naysayers a vote. Make a list of the naysayers and champions in your life. Keep these lists where you can refer to them.

As my mother used to say, "Don't pay attention to them. Just keep going."

WHAT'S YOUR WHY?

Successful people are often asked *how* they reached their goals. As intriguing as this question is, the more important one is *why?*

In the story I just shared, why did I subject myself to all the "false" hopes and rejections? Why did I keep drawing and submitting my portfolio, even though the result was silence or a discouraging "no, thank you"? Moreover, why should I encourage you to put yourself through the effort, anxiety, and uncertainty of cultivating your creative gifts? There are so many obstacles, so many uncertainties, so many challenges, and so many naysayers. For those of us who seek to use our creative gifts for good—to "make a mark" on this planet and "leave it a little better having been here" (as Jim Henson once said)—why would we want to subject ourselves to the ridicule, rejection, loneliness, and uncertainty that often comes with making a dream come true?

Because we need to.

Humans are creative beings. We are born to create. Research on creativity's effect on overall well-being seems to show that humans are at their happiest when engaged in regular creative activities—of any kind. I encourage you to explore the studies we reference in the resources section, which point at a correlation between creative activities and brain health, mood, satisfaction with life, problem-solving, mental acuity, contentment, happiness, and more.

We are inherently creative, just by being human. By "creative," I mean more than creating beautiful art. Our very lives are creations, created by us. Whether consciously or not, we are creating our lives day by day and moment by moment. Shouldn't we create them with intention rather than letting life "happen to" us randomly? We have a choice: Circumstance can shape our lives for us, or we can form our own lives from what we hold dear.

MY PURPOSE STATEMENT

As I began to realize I could actively pursue the best of what life can be, I decided to create my own personal "purpose statement" to live by. I encourage you to do the same. I wanted something that would encompass everything I stood for, believed in, and continue to reach toward. Over a six-month period, this is what came to me:

I Live My Life

As a Renaissance Priest

Through My Ministry

of Creativity

Holding the Vision of

LOVE

Before the Entire World

Demonstrating That

LIFE

Is Our Only

True Work of

ART!

This statement is the guiding force of my life. I am not always successful, but the light only grows brighter within me as I move forward on the path I am called to. That light is me learning to live my life itself as an actual work of art. As you read *Qreative Evolution*, I encourage you to write your own "purpose statement" and post it in a place where you can see it often.

Some of the things you could include in your purpose statement are: the direction you discover within your heart that your life should take, the way you would like to approach your life, the people you believe you are here to influence, and the ultimate outcome you envision for your life.

A purpose statement should be flexible enough to grow

with you, so as you learn more about your purpose in life, your purpose statement will evolve with you.

HOW I RECEIVED AN IMPORTANT CONFIRMATION

In the mid-1990s I developed *Qreative Evolution* as the title for the curriculum I was envisioning if I decided to start up an art school. A comic book artist I had worked for named Neal Adams once suggested I do an online search of my name to see if anything popped up on the internet. When I finally got around to doing this, the first thing that came up was a posting for a book entitled *Creative Evolution*.

I couldn't believe it.

I stared at my computer screen for at least three hours. How in the world could the exact title I had come up with (except for the letter "Q") pop up after I searched for my name?

It turns out that in 1911, Henry Holt and Company published *Creative Evolution* by French author Henri Bergson. The authorized translation was done by a man named Arthur Mitchell. So, the search engine's algorithm brought up a page showing this book after I did a search for my name.

I took it as a sign. I purchased Bergson's book, which is about his alternative theory on biological evolution. I think about the age-old phrase, "There is more to life than meets the eye."

I am convinced that we somehow tap into

> something intangible—a kind of divine force—
> when we move toward our purpose. This kind of
> serendipity has occurred throughout my life. By
> following my heart with the encouragement and
> protection of my mother, I was tapping into the life I
> was meant to live and discovering the path that has
> led me to the writing of this book.

QREATIVE EVOLUTION: HOW IT CAME ABOUT

I conceived *Qreative Evolution* as a way to help you discover your individual wisdom as the creator of your life. It is all about love and service to self and to humanity. It is about breaking through the barriers of despair, oppression, discouragement, and confusion in yourself, and discover those you are here to connect with. *Qreative Evolution* is a way to give and receive help; a way to find the courage to fulfill your personal creative calling.

Writing this book was a tremendous challenge because I had to go back and really look at my life over a long period of time. Remembering the difficult situations and circumstances brought back some painful memories, even traumatic ones involving people I love who hurt me and the severe hardships I had to endure. Although there are still so many challenges to deal with in life, writing *Qreative Evolution* helped me to remember the many lessons I've learned that genuinely helped me through it all so that I could share them with you. Whenever people challenged my positive outlook on life, I let them know it came at a tremendous cost. It cost me having to face myself and be honest about what my negative thinking was doing to the way I lived and allowed others to treat me. It cost me having to learn, over a great deal of time, to rise to the occasion of believing there was a better way to think and live. This was a difficult departure to the way I was accustomed to thinking and believing. So, I really had to shift gears, look for sources of positive outlooks to swap with my own and others' negativity. My mother's beautiful and uplifting voice provided constant encouragement, but there were many times when her one voice would be muffled by the noise of the naysayers, doubters, and those who just didn't subscribe to the so-called "fantasy" of positive thinking.

Sometimes things were so difficult I was tempted to give up my goals and dreams, as you will soon read about. And there were so many who would contribute to that negative way of thinking. But when I shared with them how not giving up was the one thing that helped me get through those challenges, they would ask more questions and even asked for advice about things they were going through. All I could do was share my own experiences and how I was able to overcome them or see them in the light of what I could learn from them. When so many people told me, sometimes in tears, how much what I shared helped them, I felt that my stories and life experiences might be helpful as a book. And what you are reading now is the result of many people letting me know I had something real and valuable to share.

> Again, *Qreative Evolution* is about tapping into your creative wisdom, learning to live *through* it enthusiastically and courageously as the creator of your life.

So why did I change the "C" to a "Q" in "Creative"? I did it as a reminder to *question everything*. Question *any* and *all* obstructions *and* opportunities—not from a place of doubt, but to learn what is possible. Whether you call these "challenges" or "obstacles," I believe they are not happening *to* you, but *for* you. They are lessons to help you realize what is possible for you. In *Qreative Evolution* you will discover that you are a great creator. To be creative in any area of life means that the source you draw from is your very life itself. Your creative life is vital and must be respected and protected, cultivated and nurtured.

DISCOVER VS. DECIDE

You don't decide your purpose in life; you discover it. This magnificent realization came to me in my early adulthood, setting me on a path of creative possibility. If something fascinating caught my attention, I learned to recognize that I was in the process of discovering something new within myself. I was being given an opportunity to grow. This may be difficult in some ways as you navigate through the disappointments and distractions of your life. But my goal in *Qreative Evolution* is to help quicken your awareness and sharpen your ability to "listen" to the promptings your own heart is giving you toward the true purpose of your life.

Discovering your innate creative gift is different than deciding what gift you'd like to have. Discovery is sometimes difficult in a noisy world. Discovery requires listening to oneself, and following the prompts given you by that still, small voice inside. It is a process of uncovering—and celebrating—the gift that you've carried with you since birth.

Discovery, not decision. No one is meant to figure things out in life, even though we are told from childhood that we need to "figure things out." I believe that no one can know enough about the future to figure anything out. Your life's purpose is all guesswork unless you go within to discover why you are here. Your purpose will be revealed to you over time as you listen to, and *then* follow your own heart.

CREATE YOUR OWN CURRICULUM

A defining statement for *Qreative Evolution* is "the intimate practice of creative fulfillment through guided self-education." You'll notice that "intimate" appears here and in many of the chapters. I use "intimate" to mean a deep willingness to meet our creative selves in a way we have never seen within ourselves. *Qreative Evolution* is designed to support you in developing your own ever-evolving creative curriculum. By designing your plan of study, you will discover your own fundamentals that will, in turn, help you grow as an artist. I am here to assist you, but ultimately *you* are the one discovering your creativity and using it to guide *your own* life.

As I have said before, creativity is deeply ingrained in the human spirit. It is not reserved just for people who work in artistic fields. Accessing it freely and frequently is crucial to how we live each day. It is self-sabotage to ignore the creative spirit that I believe is the very source of wisdom within us all.

Some people fight—or ignore or deny—the creativity that seeks to guide and support them. So many people consider creativity either a frivolous "extra" or a gift that only "creative types" have access to. This is a learned negative belief. You, however, are here with me, which says you are open to finding and using your creativity to shape your life.

A barista at my local Starbucks confided in me one day about her dreams of becoming a nurse, but she

felt she was too old. "You're getting older anyway,"
I told her. "So why not grow older in the direction
you want to go in, rather than a direction you don't
want to go in?" She had allowed the naysayers
in her life (and in her head) to tell her that she
was too old to return to school and get a nursing
degree. Over time, I continued to remind her of her
life's true purpose, the one that lit her up whenever
she spoke about it. One day I went in and she was
happier than I had ever seen her. She told me she
had enrolled in nursing school. A year after that, I
didn't see her at Starbucks anymore because she
had fully committed to becoming a full-time nurse.

As I've said, the naysayers don't get a vote. When something
is revealed to us, it wants to be born. *Qreative Evolution* is a way
to help you realize these dreams.

BEING CREATIVELY INTENTIONAL

You have probably heard someone claim that they "wear many
hats." You may have even said this yourself. It refers to the various—and often wildly different—activities and obligations
most of us take part in each day. If I used the word "role," you
would know exactly what I was referring to. However, I don't
believe "role" is supportive of a creative life. Think about it. The
word "role" suggests "acting" out a part rather than experiencing
something, whether that something is a daily task (like cleaning
the sink or taking a child to school) or part of a calling (such as
painting a mural, designing a medical laser, or creating a playground) that one has willingly accepted.

When you consider that your life is composed of a series of moments that you have been entrusted with, you utilize your powers of attention, which in turn grows your creativity. This is the main reason why I use the word "trusts" rather than "roles" when considering what I am responsible for in my life. This encourages me to continuously rise to the occasion of whoever or whatever I am engaging with at any given moment.

> Has there been anyone or anything that has changed you? Take a moment and think about these instances more intimately.

Each moment you have in your life is a trust. Living in the moment allows you to live genuinely so creativity can flow. People, places, and things have been entrusted to you so you can focus on them with deliberate intention.

THE PURPOSE REVEALED IN CHILDHOOD

It is generally acknowledged that a child's first few years are a formative time of exploration, learning, and skill-building. According to the American Academy of Pediatrics (AAP), by age three, a child's brain will have grown to 80 percent of its adult size. By age five, it will be 90 percent of its adult size. "The first thousand days of life are a critical and important period of development," the AAP's website reports. I am not a doctor or early childhood expert, but as a father I believe that the sixth year in a child's development is a launchpad. It's the year when self-awareness and independent evolutionary thinking begin. I was six when I discovered my own creative possibilities through seeing Jim Henson with a

Muppet on his hand, who happened to be Kermit (though, not yet a frog).

When my beloved son, Michaelanthony, was six years old, he began asking me questions about his purpose in life, questions that were beyond his years. He was a brilliant child (who is now a brilliant adult). Children in general are capable of so much more than we give them credit for, and they believe it. But many times overprotective parents and society dilute their potential. This, unfortunately, can happen even in school, the very place where children are sent to be educated.

Although his mother and I didn't always agree on how to raise Michaelanthony, we were fortunate to find a pediatrician who told me very firmly, "Don't get in his way. Just observe him, try to keep up with him, and support him through all the things he shows a genuine interest in. But stay out of his way." I, for one, was intimidated by raising this child "right." So, I immersed my baby boy in love while simultaneously "staying out of his way."

When Michaelanthony was a newborn, I insisted on doing all of his 2:00 a.m. feedings (his mother didn't object at all). This was our *magic time*; the time we truly bonded. During those wee morning hours, I looked into his eyes while I fed him. I talked to him and told him he was a champion and a genius and a great and powerful person. I told him he would get a full college scholarship one day to the college of his choice and he would travel the world. I told him I loved and adored him and that I was grateful to be his dad and have him as my son. He was just a couple of weeks old when I started doing this—so tiny and precious and beautiful. He would look into my eyes and listen to every word I said. I knew that he understood and somehow believed me.

And he did.

Michaelanthony traveled through Asia at fourteen years old. Two years later, he toured Europe. Both trips came by way of Dwight D. Eisenhower's People to People International Program. After graduating from high school with honors, Michaelanthony earned a full scholarship to Cooper Union, one of the world's most difficult art schools to get into. My son remains one of my chief creative counselors and greatest teachers, and the following lesson is among the most important eye-openers of my life.

Before leaving for elementary school each morning, Michaelanthony and I would have what was almost like a party. First, we would make breakfast together. One of his favorites was "eggs in a frame" (a variation on what our British friends call "toad in a hole"). We'd start by pressing a drinking glass into a slice of bread to make a hole and then putting the bread in a warmed skillet and cracking an egg into the hole, cooking it over easy. After eating, I would dress him in his school uniform and we'd packed his lunch box together, singing along as we went. We'd watch *Inspector Gadget* while I combed his hair. What I was trying to teach him was to enjoy each moment, starting with the beginning of each day.

I soon discovered how completely my son embraced this. One morning, I woke up feeling anxious about some unfinished work. As Michaelanthony and I walked to school, all I could think about was getting back to my desk.

Michaelanthony gently said, "Look, Dad . . . morning glories." They were his favorite flowers.

"Yes. That's nice, Chief," I said distractedly.

Suddenly he stopped and yanked my hand. "No, Dad," he said authoritatively. "Don't you miss this!"

Michaelanthony woke me from my distraction by reminding me to enjoy that moment. But he did more than that; he helped me realize that I was allowing my worry to steal this moment, a precious moment of my life. Even though Michaelanthony is now a grown man, I remember his lesson to "not miss" the beauty around me—especially when I pass morning glories.

> What special things do you think you may be missing in your life because you are distracted or afraid? How can you "wake up" to the beautiful lessons and opportunities around you?

THE REWARDS OF PERSEVERANCE

Here is a story about being awake to the kind of beautiful gifts that might be hidden in plain sight. I believe that my art career started with a twenty-five-cent comic book illustrated by a man named Neal Adams. In the late 1960s and throughout the 1970s, Neal Adams's work was widely recognized as revolutionary in the world of comic art. One of the things Neal is celebrated for is relaunching Batman as the cool, dark, complicated hero he is known as today. It would be an understatement to say that Neal Adams's work was behind my childhood dream of becoming an artist.

I have always loved comic books. When I was a child, I didn't read them as much as I studied the artwork. One day, when I was eleven years old, my sisters and I went on an outing to Prospect Park in Brooklyn. While my sisters were shopping, I went to the back of the store to look at the comic books. As I was scanning them, I spotted one that was strikingly different than any comic book I had ever seen. It was an issue of *Green Lantern and Green Arrow*, number 85, published in 1971. The story was entitled "Snowbirds Don't Fly." The artwork rather than the story, however, is what caught my attention. The level of detail was magnificent. *Why on earth would anyone put such effort into a comic book?* I thought. From the lighting to the action, the drawing was so lifelike it seemed I was watching a movie rather than looking at a comic book.

One panel in particular grabbed my attention. The background of the scene included Green Arrow, standing in front of two drug addicts and Green Lantern while talking to his ward Speedy. In the foreground was a close-up drawing of a rhinoceros pen set, beautifully lit and composed. Two detailed rhinos and two pens between them were all gorgeously rendered. The reason I found this so fascinating is because it really had absolutely nothing to do with the story. It's like Neal Adams just wanted to "show off" just how realistically he could draw. And drawing this item in such a close-up view made sure no one would miss this level of artistry and skill.

I had to have this comic book even though it cost more than the usual ones. When I asked my sister, Juanita, for the money she was shocked. "Twenty-five cents for *one* comic book?" she asked incredulously. Back then, twenty-five cents was the price of a slice of pizza. She reluctantly bought it for me along with the pizza slice.

I pored over that comic book as if it was food—and for me it was. It fed my artistic spirit like nothing I had ever encountered. After a while I made an amazing discovery: There was a hidden message from Neal Adams that I believed was just for me. On the first page of the comic book, Neal Adams had drawn a pub with a sign above the door that read, "LOUIS'S BAR." I felt this message was telling me, "Louis, this is your bar. This is your high standard. Reach for it." I started copying images from that comic book so I could learn from Neal Adams. From then on, I collected as much of his work as I could get my hands on.

Shortly after that, in junior high school, I knew I wanted to become a comic book artist like Neal Adams. Unfortunately, I encountered discouragement from everyone around me. Some of my family members would make fun of me, or my friends would be under my bedroom window yelling at me to stop wasting my time drawing and come out to play touch football. The one voice of encouragement was my mother's. Although she didn't know how to specifically encourage me, she believed in my talent. Once, she even borrowed fifty dollars (a lot of money in the 1970s!) to pay for several back-issue comic books I wanted. No other adult at the time encouraged my dream of illustrating comic books . . . until I met my eighth-grade art teacher, Mrs. Landau.

Mrs. Landau brought in all kinds of art books, showed us some of her own work, and spoke about art with an enthusiasm that was infectious. The variety of art she exposed me to was enlightening. I remember when she brought in a book of pencil drawings by Andrew Wyeth. I was riveted by the love he showed through his pencil. Seeing his work increased my love for drawing more than I can articulate.

The more Mrs. Landau expressed her enthusiasm for art, the more mine grew. The more my enthusiasm grew, the more I wanted to become an artist. The more I wanted to become an artist, the more I wanted to ask Mrs. Landau to help me. I was frightened to admit to anyone but my mother my dream of illustrating comics, because of the discouragement I had received (and was still receiving) from the naysayers (many of whom were my cousins and other kids from the neighborhood). But I longed to share my yearning to be a comic book artist with Mrs. Landau. At some point, this longing became greater than any fear I had of being looked down on.

I was *shocked* when Mrs. Landau said, "Why don't you bring me some examples of the comic books that you like?" Other than my mother, no one had ever taken such interest in my dreams. But Mrs. Landau's encouragement didn't stop there. I brought her my very favorite comic book, that same *Green Lantern and Green Arrow,* number 85. When I handed it to her, I was even more amazed at what happened next.

"Let me show you something," Mrs. Landau said. She pulled out a book of Michelangelo's artwork. Then she said, "See how this comic book artist draws the muscles of the body? He studied the same thing that Michelangelo studied in order to draw the body so well. It's called 'anatomy.' You can study it and learn how to become a great artist, too."

I was grateful that Mrs. Landau took comic book art so seriously that she compared the work of Neal Adams with the work of Michelangelo. That generous act of kindness nurtured the love of art that would live within me for the rest of my life. She remains my greatest art teacher—actually, my greatest *teacher*—of all time.

Because of Mrs. Landau's loving encouragement, I learned everything I could about comic book production. Generally, comic books are made in a very specific way. Someone writes the story, a penciller draws it, and an inker "inks" what the penciller created. After being introduced to Andrew Wyeth's work by Mrs. Landau, pencil drawing had become my favorite artistic medium. Even though Neal Adams was a phenomenal penciller, he was also an equally phenomenal inker, as demonstrated in "Snowbirds Don't Fly." I was feeling so good about my drawing skills that I even joked to my friends, "One day, Neal Adams is going to ink my pencils." Thanks to my mom and Mrs. Landau, my confidence was growing enough to start speaking my dreams aloud. For me, confidence was something so foreign because of how low mine was. But Mrs. Landau and my mother revealed confidence as the part of me that was capable of learning and growing in the direction of improving myself. We will take a deeper look at confidence and how to get it later in this chapter. The focus here is on who might be the source of helping you toward your own confidence.

> Do you remember your own most influential teachers? Which ones made the most impact on your life and why?

After I graduated from middle school and started high school, I got a job at the New York Comic Art Gallery, which had just opened near my school. I was paid in comic books because the owner, a wonderful man named Mark Rindner, couldn't hire anyone for pay yet. But I *had* to work there. He saw how much I wanted to enter the world of comic books, so he hired me that day.

Working there would get me into a comic book convention for free. It was my very first convention and I was thrilled. It took up three giant ballrooms at the Hotel Pennsylvania, across the street from Madison Square Garden. When I walked from the main ballroom to the second one, who was standing right in the middle of the room but Neal Adams himself! I recognized him from pictures I had seen in comic books and fan magazines. I approached him and asked him to sign *The Neal Adams Treasury* fan book I had just purchased. As he checked his pockets, I realized he didn't have a pen.

"I have a pen," I said quickly. "I'll be right back." I ran as fast as I could back to the first ballroom to get my pen, whispering to myself, "Oh, please wait . . . please don't leave."

When I returned, there he was. He signed my book and walked off. I had met my hero. And I still have that very same book.

A few months later while I was working at the gallery, Mark Rindner told me that a friend of his was looking for an assistant to help him in his studio. It was Howard Chaykin. Among many other things, he would become the first *Star Wars* comic book artist. At that time, however, I wasn't familiar with his work. (All I cared about was Neal Adams.) I realized that even though I didn't understand Howard's work, he was a professional in the industry that I wanted to work in. So I went for the interview. He loved my work and offered me a job as his assistant. I learned so much from him *and* became a fan once I was exposed to his work.

One day, as I was preparing to go home, he said to me, "Hey, on the first Friday of every month, all the comic book artists in New York City have a 'First Friday Party' at one of our homes. The next one is tomorrow. You wanna come?"

I was beyond excited. After I stuttered yes, Howard told me, "By the way . . . this one is at Neal Adams's house."

Howard told me to bring my sketchbooks to show Neal. This

terrified me. I had always heard how hard Neal Adams was on other artists because of his exceedingly high standards. Nevertheless, I reluctantly brought three of my sketchbooks and hoped for the best. I knew in my heart that if Neal Adams didn't like my work it would crush me, but I was not going to miss a chance to go to Neal Adams's house. When I got there, I was greeted by Neal's daughter, Kris. I was a shy seventeen-year-old who wasn't comfortable approaching the other guests, but Kris was nice to me and handed me a plate of lasagna. I sat in a corner, eating Kris's amazing lasagna and glancing at the television, as many of the country's most famous comic book artists socialized around me.

When Howard Chaykin showed up, he didn't waste a second. He asked if I had brought my work, and I handed him my sketchbooks. He kneeled in front of Neal, who was sitting on the couch across from me, and began to flip through my work.

"Look how great this kid is at only seventeen years old," Howard explained, pointing to various drawings.

Neal looked at all three sketchbooks, backward and forward, three times over. He finally stopped and looked at me. "You know, I have been sitting on a series of scripts. I haven't found anyone that I thought could handle them. But I think you can. Come up to Continuity tomorrow"—this was his art studio—"and I'll get you started on the project."

My hero had hired me on the spot. I thanked him politely and said I would be there at 10:00 a.m. as requested. And then I left. I was *exploding* inside and could not contain it. I had to get out of there immediately before I collapsed.

When I got down to the street I began to scream as loud as I could, "Neal Adams just hired me on the spot! I work for Neal Adams!"

I didn't care how stupid I looked or what anyone thought. I had just been hired by my hero.

The comic book series Adams assigned me was called *Tippie Toe Jones*, written by Lindley Farley. I worked on this series for over three years. Tippie Toe Jones was a cartoon character who lived in the real world. So, I was required to draw in a cartoon style for the main character and draw everything else in a realistic style. And guess what? After only a year, *Neal Adams was inking my pencils!*

> What I had been jokingly dreaming of became a reality and taught me a valuable lesson: Dreams are not fantasies. Dreams are seeds.

When this first dream of mine came true, it taught me to believe in things that the naysayers said were impossible. Working for Neal Adams was only my first big dream that came true. There would be more to come, many of which would surpass anything I could imagine. Somehow—without even realizing it—I had begun my journey as a lifelong student of myself, my creativity, and of humanity. While on this path, I learned something that changed how I viewed my own life purpose. This truth would ignite my life with motivation, enthusiasm, and a deep sense of comfort.

REMEMBER, YOU DON'T DECIDE YOUR PURPOSE IN LIFE, YOU DISCOVER IT

This magnificent realization set me on a path that was brand new to me. If something wonderfully creative was prompting me toward it, I learned to recognize that I was in the process of discovering something new within myself—an opportunity to grow. With that thought in mind, I need to address a particular pet peeve of mine here.

So many people tell children that they can be anything they want to be. But this is wrong. This pressures them into thinking they have to figure out what they should do. We need to tell them the truth: that they can become whatever they *discover* they are meant to be by searching and following their own hearts for what is already within them. They just have to go inside to get it and listen to the desires of their own hearts.

Remember, this is about discovery, not decision.

No one is meant to figure things out in life, even though we are told that we are. Again, no one is truly capable of knowing enough about the future to figure anything out. It is all guesswork unless you go within to discover it. It will be revealed to you over time as you are guided through the process of discovering who you are. We are meant to take the journey and listen from within. What do you hear when you listen to your heart? What discoveries are revealed? These questions will lead you to what I call "The Artlife."

THE ARTLIFE

What kind of creative person are you? What do you love to do, and how do you love to do it? Who supports you best? Whom do you support? What do you feel your creative purpose is in this world? Your artlife is another way to say "your unique life as a creative human."

What is the essence of your own artlife? Is it going to the museum? Traveling to the Galapagos Islands? Is it simply sitting with your sketchbook and drawing image after image with no hesitation? Or is it privately dancing in your bedroom? Whatever it is, your artlife deserves to be celebrated, indulged, and hedonistically pursued. Your Artlife requires that you feed yourself with those things that will generate more of the greatness that will support both yourself and humanity as a whole. In return, your creative spirit will move you toward the life-affirming manifestations that await you. Your artlife is healthy. It is not indulging in things that will hurt, destroy, distract, or pollute you, your potential, or anyone else's. This is why it is vital to examine the motives behind your desires, as well as how you approach them. Since I coined the term "artlife," I am taking the initiative to define it as "seeking the good you can bring forth to remind others that we are here as creators, not destroyers."

As you live your personal artlife, you will delve deeply into the very things that ignite and inspire you. Remember: There is no one more qualified than you to know what will stimulate, encourage, challenge, and grow you.

QREATIVE EVOLUTION'S SIX EVOLUTIONARY TRUSTS

Each chapter of *Qreative Evolution* is based on one of "The Six Evolutionary Trusts." You'll learn more about each one of these "trusts" in the pages ahead. These supports create a sense of ease around creative living. You will recognize the unique-to-you champions and motivators who will help you grow your creativity. Likewise, you'll grow aware of elements (people, activities, places, thought patterns, and more) that can hinder (or enhance) your personal creativity.

These Six Evolutionary Trusts are:

1. The Creative Journey: You discover you genuinely are a creative person, regardless of what evidence you have yet found. By trusting this is true, you will discover clues regarding your calling and your purpose. You meet your true self—perhaps for the first time—and courageously value your entire life as your true work of art. The light of your inspiration is turned on. I call this *Qreative Evolution*.

2. Wisdom, or Expanding the Understanding of Your Gift: You begin discovering more and more evidence of your creativity. You commit to your creative journey and have faith that your gifts will be revealed as you continue to explore what motivates you and brings you joy. I call this *Evolutionary Wisdom*.

3. Awareness and Identifying Your Unique Gifts: Awareness of your creativity allows you to excel in creating your life. As you move forward on your creative path, you will discover your own unique creative gifts. Empowered by what you learn, you will become bolder in sharing your abilities with others. I call this *Evolutionary Knowledge*.

4. Purpose: You trust and act on your own ideas as they come to you. You also realize what inspires you, and how. You realize that in order for something to attract your attention, it must be a reflection of not only your talents, but who you are deep within. I call this *Evolutionary Practice*.

5. Tribal Connections: Needing support from others does not make you weak, nor is it something to be

embarrassed about. Among the most important discoveries you can make when designing your life is to
discover who belongs in it, who does not belong, and
whose life you are meant to be in. Receiving and giving
support is a form of reciprocity that regenerates not just
your own creative energy but improves the flow of everyone's creativity. Think of the saying, "a rising tide lifts
all boats." Support of all types (emotional, intellectual,
career, and more) is meant for you to access whenever
you want to reach out for it. In accepting and giving
support, your own humanity rises to an astounding level
of flowing creativity. I call this *Evolutionary Fellowship*.

6. Creating Your Life with Enthusiasm: As you become
comfortable with your creative gifts—and realize that
your life is your ultimate creation—you experience a
shift in mindset. In other words, living on purpose, with
purpose, and within your purpose. Observe where your
various gifts belong and where they will flourish. Doing
the right thing at the wrong time, just like planting the
right seed in the wrong soil, helps no one. In the right
(for you) place, in the right (for you) time, your ambi-
tions send your creativity soaring like an eagle in flight.
I call this *Transcendent Qreativity*.

THE MYTH OF THE CREATIVE BLOCK

There are necessary periods of incubation when you are in the
creative process. Sometimes these quiet periods are an indicator that you may need more information or an extended time
of meditation before you begin a project. Or, a feeling of being
stuck can indicate that you may be neglecting part of your artlife.

Perhaps you are being called to stop and feed your inner creative resources before you can proceed. Perhaps you might go see a play or visit a museum. Deep down, you know what will stimulate you better than anyone else can suggest. You may be in need of some vital information that will ignite or jolt your creativity. None of these periods, however, are creative blocks. They are simply messages from your soul that your creative spirit needs something.

The ultimate proof that there are no creative blocks is the idea of the "block" itself. You have to *create* the block and empower it before it can become a real thing. The block you believe in was *created by you*. Therefore, through the process of living your artlife, you can disconnect from this self-created block, honor your creative process, and continue on after you've discovered what your artlife is craving. Getting away from your regular environment and seeing life afresh can be tremendously helpful. Take a simple walk in a new neighborhood, or go as far as embarking on a long journey. The "block" is a hunger pang. You will discover what "food" will satisfy it when you step away from your routine environment and listen to your heart. The next time you feel creatively frozen in place, resist the urge to power through. Instead, respect your creativity, and stop and give yourself what your creative spirit is asking for.

THE SEVEN AREAS OF A QREATIVE LIFE

There are fundamental areas of life that, when attended to, help to create a deep sense of well-being. From this place, you experience emotional as well as practical safety, which in turn makes it easy to let your creativity flow freely. While these are certainly not new concepts, I share them here because *Qreative*

Evolution is a book about discovering and growing your creativity by considering familiar ideas in new and unique ways. These important areas of your life act as a scaffolding, giving your life shape and stability. I call this type of supportive structure a "launchpad" because it allows your creativity to begin flowing unencumbered, wherever makes sense for you. Everything you notice, feel, think about, experience—everything (and everyone!) that passes through your life—helps you launch and then progress through your creative life.

Below are the Seven Areas of a Qreative Life that I feel deserve direct attention:

1. Spirit—Cultivate a relationship with yourself. Pause each day to check in with yourself and your higher power. Explore your progress, evaluate who you are, affirm your purpose for being here. Truly understanding yourself helps you become your own best friend and advocate.

2. Soul—Feed your soul by immersing yourself in creative activities and resources. Notice the creativity of others and allow it to inform and inspire you. Read books, study art, watch a play or a dance performance, listen to live (or recorded) music, look at interesting buildings, and immerse yourself in the inspiration all around you. Deliberately cultivating your "thoughtlife"—the life you live within your thoughts—allows your thoughts to manifest externally in your everyday world.

3. Body—We often think of the body as separate from the mind. What I have found, however, is that a well-cared-for body leads to a focused, agile brain. The brain and body are connected through neural transmitters, which is why

you may hear health experts talk about the "mind-body connection." Honor your body as your creativity partner. As you healthfully feed, train, recuperate, and strengthen your body, it offers you the vitality to access what you are called to creatively do. This is true health.

4. Social—Humans are social beings, who are healthiest when they are in regular contact with others. Make time to connect with those whom you share a mutual love of creativity and life. These are individuals who will give you perspective, expose you to different ways of thinking, and encourage you to grow further. Discover your tribe carefully. You may have heard the phrase "You are the average of the five people you spend the most time with." This quote (attributed to motivational speaker Jim Rohn) is based on research by Harvard psychologist Dr. David McClelland, which found that 95 percent of someone's success in various areas (health, finances, etc.) is determined by their social circle. With this in mind, avoid naysayers and the revealed enemies of your calling.

5. Financial—Money allows you to live your life so that you can honor and fund your creativity. The pursuit of money should never be your motivator, but you must support yourself in order to live. Practice financial self-care by earning money, setting funds aside for both current necessities and the future, paying your debts, and living within your means. Acquire and manage the financial resources necessary for you to honor what you are creatively called to do.

6. Professional—When we accept the call of a creative life, we may work in a position that does not showcase our

artistic gifts. Regardless of your current employment, cultivate the work ethic and the standards necessary to reap the harvest of your gifts with enthusiasm. As you grow creatively, your ideal work will be revealed, allowing you to move into employment that aligns with your life's purpose. The people and opportunities that you are meant to have in your life will be attracted to you through what you reveal in your talents and skills.

7. Devotional—There is so much more to this world than meets the eye. One of the most neglected areas of human life is spiritual enlightenment. The mysteries of life can offer genuine wisdom when explored beyond our conventional thinking. Meditation, prayer, reflection—these are vital elements of self-evaluation, which keep us on our true path, while helping us return to it when we stray.

THE TRUE PATH TO CONFIDENCE

I have taken part in many panel discussions, speaking to people of all ages and walks of life. One question always comes up, usually asked by someone who is really struggling: "What do I do if I don't have the confidence to believe in myself?"

For some reason, every time I have been on a panel, I am always the last in the line of speakers. It feels like a divine appointment for me, because being the last speaker to answer any given question allows me to hear my colleagues' thoughts on the matter. Unfortunately, when it comes to self-esteem, most of them give just the answer that you'd expect: "You should feel confident about yourself. You should believe in your talents and abilities and have confidence in them." As panelist after panelist repeats some variation of this standard and unhelpful advice, I look out at the audience and recognize the frustrated facial expressions of those who struggle with a lack of confidence.

Lack of confidence is a tremendous albatross around the collective neck of humanity. It deserves a truer, more helpful solution than "just *be* confident."

There was a time in my early life when I desperately needed an answer to this question. No one ever gave me that answer, which is why I was determined to find a *real* answer. Looking over my own life, I thought about how I went from a beginning artist with low self-esteem, to the confident person I am now. How did this happen for me? How did I get to a place where I can speak up, seize professional opportunities, address large audiences, appear on television, offer up my opinions, and ask for advice without feeling embarrassed or anxious? As I investigated my own life to learn how I became so confident, I discovered an answer that I believe is true for absolutely everyone: Commitment. Commitment creates confidence.

When I was studying life drawing and anatomy early in my career, it was extremely frustrating. Anatomy is very difficult to learn. As I drew, struggling to understand what was in my anatomy books, I would suddenly crumple up what I had done and throw it across the room. But I *loved* to draw and studied to get better. Sometimes I would find the crumpled-up paper and look at it again, smooth it out as much as I could, and keep it for examination later. Even though I didn't like what I was doing early on, I kept drawing. I kept studying the anatomy books and going to the Art Students League for life drawing classes.

It was a few years before I realized I wasn't struggling with a lack of confidence in my anatomy studies as much anymore.

I was enjoying the drawing and, although I was still challenged with understanding how the human body relates to itself and how proportions worked, I was not experiencing the anxiety that I had before. I pushed myself to enter my drawings in shows. They were getting so much better and receiving special acknowledgments. Without even knowing it, I became very confident with my anatomy and life drawings. Because I stayed committed to drawing and studying anatomy, I cultivated the ever-increasing confidence that I enjoy to this very day.

That's when it hit me: The cure for lack of confidence was commitment, or the willingness to study daily—for years, if need be—until a skill became second nature. Because commitment increased my artistic confidence, I decided to apply it to other areas in my life where I struggled with a lack of confidence. I found that the more committed I was to an area, the more confident I became. That's how I became a public speaker, a teacher, a mentor, and even a writer. Confidence is not like a light switch to flip on whenever it's needed. That's why those audience members frowned or rolled their eyes when they were told that they should just "be confident." It made them feel broken, as if something was wrong with them because they couldn't just "turn on the confidence." The truth is that *confidence is the by-product of commitment.* Whenever I said that commitment is the key to confidence, the person who had asked about their lack of it would beam and sometimes even shed a tear.

Confidence is a journey that takes time. Confidence must also be built upon. Practicing is crucial to not only becoming more confident but also in staying confident. Confidence can be lost if it isn't fed through practice. Even the greatest athletes and musicians continue to practice and study what they do or they get "rusty," which leads to a dwindling confidence.

As you grow and change, your self-esteem will grow with you. It will evolve with you as you increase in knowledge and wisdom. Stay committed to your *Qreative Evolution*. Cultivate, with every tool within and around you, your creative gift. Through what you love, you discover your gifts and through your gifts, you discover your purpose in life.

CHAPTER ONE GUIDED SELF-EDUCATION INQUIRY: YOUR QREATIVE EVOLUTION

Welcome to the close of Chapter One. After each chapter, you will find an interactive activity designed to draw your attention to your creative self. Think of these as guided self-education inquiries.

An inquiry is a multistep process of learning that begins when you notice something in the physical world or within yourself. After observing the thing and exploring elements connected with the thing, you then ask questions that will lead to deeper discoveries and new understanding.

These post-chapter activities can create seismic shifts in the way you see yourself and your journey. It is vital that you answer these questions completely and with deep and total honesty. This may take a while, and you may find yourself needing to break up the question-answering into several sittings. That is okay; completing the post-chapter activities fully will change your life.

If, on your first attempt, you struggle to answer a question, don't worry, just meditate on it until you get a substantial answer. Take all the time you need to answer each question thoroughly and honestly. Take comfort in knowing that this is exclusively for you and no one else will see your answers.

Because *Qreative Evolution* is meant to be a lifelong guide, you will want to refer back to your answers. You may also want to periodically reanswer each chapter's inquiries so you can gauge your progress over time. Revisiting these activities should become a tradition that you engage in monthly or yearly—however often you feel will help you create and create the life you are meant to live (and love).

Studies have shown that writing by hand activates many brain functions, from problem-solving to memorization. It also helps us generate ideas and allows us to access deep personal thoughts and memories. (One of the most recent of these studies was performed by the Norwegian University of Science and Technology on preteens and adults, and the results were published in the July 28, 2020, issue of *Frontiers in Psychology*.) Pen and paper, such as a notepad or paper notebook, are highly recommended. I suggest a looseleaf binder because of the ability to remove pages as needed, but please use whatever will encourage you to explore the following questions toward your Qreative Evolution:

1. Where do you lack confidence and why? How can you use commitment to change that?

2. Describe your greatest aspiration in minute detail. Give yourself time to delve deeply into yourself. This is your opportunity to explore those creative desires, as well as your many dreams, that you have for yourself. This is not the place for negativity. Therefore, I ask you to ignore any doubts, fears, people, or situations that will limit this vital part of your Qreative Evolution.

3. What do you believe is the great calling and purpose of your life?

4. What in your life brings you the greatest joy?

5. What are you particularly good at? What comes easily to you?

6. What unique talents, gifts, and strengths do you possess?

7. What compliments do you receive on a regular basis?

8. When you were a child, what did you want to be?

9. What inspires you the most? What holds your interest most strongly?

10. What is the greatest and deepest desire of your heart?

11. What, at this point in your life, is of the single most importance to you?

Chapter Two

EVOLUTIONARY WISDOM

Having a "calling" is a time-honored idea that reaches far back into human history. It explains the feeling of purpose many of us experience regarding our gifts. A calling is not something that you *choose* to do. It is something you are *meant* to do. You can have one calling or many. These callings may be professional, personal, social, spiritual, artistic, academic, or intellectual in nature. Getting to that place of wisdom is a process of discovery, which is powered by your growing awareness of your gifts. In this chapter, we examine what the term "calling" means, and its relationship to the word "wisdom."

Getting the job at Sesame Workshop was, as I have mentioned before, a dream come true. There was an atmosphere of joy that permeated the company, even when the work was extremely intense and the schedules very tight. I was determined to make the absolute most of this opportunity each and every day. Part of making the most of this experience included supporting my coworkers. I felt a calling to help support the people in my life.

Tom Peters is one of my favorite business gurus. I once heard him say that the best way to succeed at the "bottom line" (finances) is to make sure you take excellent care of the "top line" (employees). This made sense to me. Whatever your goal is, it's the people who help you get there; they should never be taken for granted.

Many of my coworkers would come to my small office to speak with me about work, personal projects, and life in general. In fact, at one point my coworkers were affectionately calling me "The Pastor of *Sesame Street*." The only challenge was when people shared extremely painful life moments, like when someone's sister was diagnosed with breast cancer or someone's brother and sister-in-law had a miscarriage. I reminded people that I was not really a pastor and that they should bring these sensitive issues to a professional counselor. Without exception, however, my beloved coworkers would each say in their individual ways, "Oh, Louis, I just feel better talking to you about this. I'm not asking anything of you but your trusted ear and the comfort of your office."

I learned that when people are treated with respect and given a genuine safe place to speak, they truly appreciate it. It was never my intention to be available for everyone, but I did want to be there for whomever I could. Connecting with my coworkers in this way made an already fulfilling job that much more special to me. I sensed a calling within my own heart to be the best listener and supporter that I could be. As long as I stayed on schedule with my work and did the best I could on all that I was responsible for, I believed supporting my coworkers was the right thing to do.

The workload at *Sesame Street* was heavy, and we reached a

point where we needed additional help. My supervisor, whom I truly admired and loved working under, was trying to hire an extra artist. The salary for this person was going to be substantial because we needed an experienced artist who could hit the ground running and didn't require a long season of training. One morning my supervisor came into my office. She explained that if the finance manager saw all these people visiting me each day, he would not be convinced we needed more help and would therefore not approve the funds for a new artist.

My work was never late. In fact, many times I would be ahead of schedule on my projects. I reminded my supervisor of this, appealing to her own sense of humanity. She said kindly but firmly that what I was doing wasn't part of my job and could keep our department from growing as we needed to. So, I reluctantly—but respectfully—agreed to stop speaking with people during our usual working hours and only in the mornings or after work. The only problem was that I knew most of them didn't come in early or stay late because of the very challenges they wanted to share with me. I went back to my office feeling discouraged.

Within fifteen minutes of my returning to my office, the finance manager himself came to me and asked what I was doing. I nervously told him I was just in a meeting with my supervisor and was about to get back on one of my projects. Then he asked me something that I was not expecting. "You sent your son to China for a summer didn't you?"

I said, "Yes, I did because he earned it as part of a special program at his junior high school. Why do you ask?"

This tall, serious businessman dressed in a beautiful, expensive suit suddenly looked shaken. "Louis, you sent your son halfway across the world for an entire summer. I'm about to send my son across the country, just to California, for two weeks and I am a wreck. Can I please sit and speak with you about how you coped? I'm going crazy."

The very person my supervisor wanted to keep from seeing me supporting others was the person who came to me in the most vulnerable way of all (and only a few minutes after my supervisor had admonished me). The finance manager poured his heart out to me and was even a bit choked up. I was able to share my own challenges with him, and my resolutions about sending my son overseas. As he stood up to leave, he gave me a hug and told me what a great help I had been to him.

I returned to my supervisor's office to share what had just happened. Without gloating, I reassured her that all was good between our department and the finance manager, and she then apologized for losing sight of the people-to-people interactions that fuel the human creativity at Sesame Workshop.

I can't describe the feeling of validation I felt, not in an arrogant way, but in gratitude. I had begun to question my calling of supporting my coworkers. But afterward, I believe it was divinely ordered for me to be reprimanded so that my calling of listening to others could be immediately revealed and validated as part of my mission at work and in life. In that moment, I recognized the call to encourage and support anyone that I was able to. Ultimately, that situation and so many others led me to write this book.

RISE TO THE CALL

Why does it matter whether or not a person has a calling? A person can live a long, healthy, and relatively happy life without knowing their calling. But their life can be even more satisfying, inspiring, and impactful when they follow the wisdom that a calling brings.

Hundreds of studies on the effects of vocational and personal callings have been written over the last three decades. One of these many studies, entitled "Purpose in Life and Positive Health Outcomes Among Older Adults" found that individuals who felt that they were "living their purpose" scored 54.7 percent higher on health, well-being, and happiness surveys than those who were not living their purpose.

Another article entitled "The Value of a Purposeful Life: Sense of Purpose Predicts Greater Income and Net Worth" published in the *Journal of Research in Personality* finds a correlation between living one's identified purpose and personal wealth. There are dozens of similar studies which conclude that individuals who have a calling, and pursue that calling, experience higher levels of happiness, contentment, social connection, creativity, well-being, and income than those who do not know (or live) their calling.

Perhaps the idea of having a "calling" is not familiar to you. A calling is an inner awareness and desire to do something, go somewhere, or help someone in a special way. Many people feel the call to become a doctor early in their lives, or later when they observe an area of health care they believe they can improve upon. Some people are called to music or teaching. My mother and I were both very young when we discovered our callings. She was eight years old when she discovered her calling to become a nurse as she played hospital with her dolls. I discovered my calling to become a Muppet artist when I was six years old. The artist Grandma Moses was called to start painting when she was well over seventy years old and continued past the age of one hundred. It's all a matter of listening to the inner call of your own heart. I believe everyone has at least one calling in their life that deserves to be discovered.

As you become more familiar with your gifts and how to share them, you will grow wiser regarding the best way for you to utilize them for the good of all. Having a calling is not only helpful in supporting others, but it also helps *you* by guiding you through the choices that appear and the discoveries you make. A calling gives you direction and the ability to genuinely say "yes" to the right things that come your way and "no" to choices that don't support your calling.

Follow your interests by following your heart and your deep inner creative desires. They will guide you to your next steps. An example from my own life is my decision, in high school, to visit a bookstore after school, where I perused the art books instead of going to McDonalds or hanging with my friends. I went into that bookstore to explore different kinds of art. Just putting myself in that environment gave me options that I didn't even know were possible for me. Think about what inspires you. Where could you go that would inspire new ideas? These ideas can reveal your next steps.

"The greatest thing a teacher can teach you is to teach yourself."

—ISAAC STERN

CHALLENGES ARE OPPORTUNITIES TO GROW

It's important to acknowledge the types of challenges you may be facing at any given time.

They are indicators of where you need to build
your strengths, what to study, who (and what) to
avoid (or approach), and what to pursue. You
will experience your own unique obstacles. Some
may seem insignificant and some gargantuan,
depending upon where you are on your path.
When faced with a hurdle, stop and think about the
lessons your challenges are offering to you.

HOW TO FIND YOUR CALLING

This advice appears throughout this book in many different ways, but the truest, most direct way of discovering your calling is to follow your heart. It will not lead you astray. Many people look to successful people and try to emulate them. Although you can learn much from people who are doing well, their callings are not your calling. Your calling is unique to you. It shapes your identity and gives you purpose. The main difference between your purpose and your calling is this: Your purpose is your "why," your callings (and yearnings) are your specific "fuel," and, additionally, your assignments are your "how."

Have you ever felt that your heart was leading you somewhere? That is usually a sign of your calling. Even if it is not your ultimate calling, it can get you moving in the right direction.

In Chapter One, I mentioned that as a child, I wanted to be like Jim Henson. I also wanted to be like comic book artist Neal Adams. However, as I continued to study and learn from these extraordinary people, I began to discover my unique desires. These led me to my own, unique path of creativity and personal fulfillment. Following my heart, even when I was afraid, helped me create the life of my dreams.

"The object of life is not to have a perfect life; it is to have a perfect sense of life that you can take with you anywhere."

—JANIS BEAUCHAMP

WORDS OF WISDOM

Throughout *Qreative Evolution* you will find quotes to inspire you. I find that reading the wisdom of others sparks my own personal wisdom. These positive messages ignite my thinking, energize me so I can continue on, show me new ways to approach a challenge, or offer up ideas that I'd never before considered. The sayings I've shared here come from my own personal "inspiration collection," a library of quotes that I keep nearby to read daily. This is also one of the ways I ignite and become more aware of my own desires and my calling. Sometimes what you hear from others awakens the desire within your own heart. That awakening can reveal elements of your calling to you.

I encourage you to keep your own library of quotes. You can start with the quotes in this book that resonate with you and expand your collection whenever you come across a quote that moves you.

Write your favorite quotes in a notebook, or

> use them as a computer screen saver. Add them to
> a vision board. Post them on a mirror. Find ways to
> collect them. Allowing yourself to be inspired daily
> by the wisdom of others is an easy and powerful
> way to feed your creativity.

LIFE WILL FIGHT TO REMIND YOU OF YOUR CALLING

So often, we become frustrated and challenged in life because we stray from our unique paths. We allow ourselves to listen to messages that deafen us to who we are and what potential we have.

As I've mentioned earlier, naysayers are a source of what can deafen our inner voice of possibilities because of the negativity they bring. This negativity can make us feel vulnerable or ashamed of our desires. It can also lead us to feel our calling is something we need to hide, or do in secret, or give up on entirely. When this happens, we become our own naysayer.

We stop attending to our calling, or we choose to reject it entirely. When this happens, life tries to get our attention so we can return to our calling. Why?

Having a calling gives shape to our lives. It gives us direction that keeps us on track. Having a sense of purpose is good for our well-being, too. In 2015, there was an investigation conducted by Michele W. Gazica and Paul E. Spector from the University of South Florida during which nearly four hundred professors from universities across the United States were asked about their commitment to a calling. After rating their physical health, mental health, career engagement, and life satisfaction, the healthiest professors were the ones who had a calling they had committed to. The least healthy were the professors who had a calling they ignored. Put another way, having a calling is healthy if you follow it but negative if you choose to ignore it.

I view it as fortunate that life makes it difficult to ignore your calling. Life will scream at you to wake up. Life will continue screaming until you rise to the standard you are being called to. In my case, life spoke to me through a great supervisor who lost sight of the deeper substance that helped me do the best job I could, which was helping others. This fed me and made me even more compassionate, so when I set my hand to draw the *Sesame Street* Muppets, I was able to deliver that compassion to children who saw my work.

We will not truly be able to find genuine comfort on any level when we ignore the call to be our best creative selves. Extreme frustration, confusion, restlessness, malaise, insomnia, discomfort, pain, and stress—these are some of the ways life alerts us. These warnings are our genuine allies. Without them, we could risk staying stuck in limbo, unaware that we are allowing the death of our true potential.

Life will not allow you to ignore your gifts without an inward challenge. As you do things that are contrary to who you are and what you are called to do, life will shake you. It will "throw wrenches into the works" and disrupt the misaligned life you may be giving in to. Life will *fight* you to get back on track. However, your current life can't even compare with the genuine sanctuary you could experience when you follow your inner calling and live your genuine life.

Imagine living a life where you rise to every occasion with clarity and hope. Where you realize that life, itself, is calling you to reach higher, dig deeper, go further. When you listen to your inner wisdom you can hear your life calling to you.

ULTIMATE DISBELIEF

What you believe about humanity at your core is what you believe about yourself. It has been said that what offends you about others is a sign of what you don't like about yourself. But what you are offended by is a hint toward something you are here to help improve upon. Any doubt you may have in humanity is a hint of any doubt you have regarding yourself. Likewise, your belief in humanity is also a clear sign of your belief in your own potential. This is why courage in your humanity—the qualities that make you human—is vital to your entire life. Spending time bravely exploring your thoughts and beliefs—about others and yourself—takes courage. What you will learn, however, will lead to wisdom—about yourself, your gifts and your life calling.

THE DECEPTION OF FAILURE

One of the most debilitating fears creative people face is the fear of failure. And yes, I am talking to you because, remember, we are all artists creating our entire lives. So this applies to us all. What is usually called "failure," however, needs to be redefined. It is *practice*; another step in your evolutionary progress.

There are some difficult situations you may need to "grow

through" before you can access a particular skill or evolve in a specific area. This growth is just one of the many progressive steps in your *Qreative Evolution*.

Many times things don't go as planned. They can even go terribly wrong. Wisdom often comes from what seem to be missteps. The problem, however, is when you consider these missteps as "failures." Perhaps you've tried to design a schedule for yourself and made it more ambitious than you were ready for. Maybe you set out to create something that you haven't yet developed the skills for. Or, as in my own case, attempt to write a book (due to peer pressure) and get it published years before I was ready. These can look like "failures" and stir up feelings of "I'm not good enough," as well as the fear of moving forward.

Yes, we do make mistakes. But what does that mean? A mistake means you took something and missed the proper way it was meant to be handled or done. Realize this and try doing it another way until you get it right. Mistakes are not a dead end. We can look *through* what are called "mistakes" with a different mindset.

We are taught to avoid mistakes. We are taught to fear failure. But these are simply temporary assumptions. Instead of looking at your missteps as mistakes and failures, look *through* them as *practice*. This takes us back to how we behave while we are on our journey.

There is something you can do to handle these fears.

Remember that the key to moving forward is to look through everything as part of your necessary process. You can choose to cultivate fear by not trying, which ultimately sends you deeper into fear. Or, you can take baby steps in the direction of progress.

You may need courage to take those small steps forward. To quote M. Scott Peck, author of *The Road Less Traveled*, "Courage is not the absence of fear; it is the making of action in spite of fear, the moving out against the resistance engendered by fear into the unknown and into the future." It is the realization that moving toward something new can be understandably frightening, then moving toward that thing anyway.

What you are here to do isn't always immediately evident. You will eventually evolve in the direction you submit to most often, be it positive or negative. Without a deliberate decision to submit to what you've discovered within yourself and the corresponding action to thrive, you will be taken up in whatever current surrounds you.

Continue courageously on your path. All the good that you want to do has enormous value. It holds a huge part of the "genetic code" of your life's purpose within it. Remember, any negative or destructive parts of your life's work are important indicators. They can reveal areas you may need to work on, get help with, or completely disregard. They should not be ignored because they are signs that your internal wisdom is communicating with you; this is your guided self-education. So you must learn to trust your own personal *Qreative Evolution* and follow the benevolence of your own heart.

PERSONAL CREATIVE FULFILLMENT

Creativity is often associated with a person's profession. However, it's important to evolve as a creative person regardless of whether or not you use your creative gifts to earn a living. Every element of your life is improved when you nurture your creativity. Creativity is a catalyst for your personal human fulfillment.

Your creative fulfillment depends upon your honest dedication to your own human growth.

The yearnings within you, the inner promptings, the unique sources of inspiration, your desires—these are all part of your creativity. They are a part of *you*. They pull you and stretch you and evolve you. No matter what anyone does to try to help you grow, it will never reach the depths within you. No one knows your inner thoughtlife or what can develop you more than you. That is why guided self-education is vital. Never let an assignment given by someone else be your only—or even the primary—challenge in creativity. Personal experience is where growth and evolution are cultivated.

FOLLOW YOUR YEARNINGS

Yearning is a "hunger" that sends you searching for your life's deep purpose, that thing in life that you absolutely must do. There are people who absolutely must run in the morning each and every day or they don't feel like themselves. Some people must write, either in their journals or work on their own manuscript. In my own experience of yearning, I absolutely must do my morning drawing practice. The rare mornings when I don't do it, I am affected throughout the day and that yearning does not leave me all day long. So, I'll stop and draw anywhere at any time. It is your contribution to life and purpose in life. It is what you are here to accomplish. I am absolutely convinced that everyone has one very specific and positive purpose to live for and assignments to accomplish in life. My heart bleeds for those who miss this in their lives, or who choose not to pursue and discover it.

Your calling cannot be decided on. It can only be discovered. What you are doing right now may not be what you are ultimately meant to do. Or it may be. You will learn what your purpose is and how to get to it as you move courageously forward. You will receive messages from your soul and directions from your own heart that will help you navigate toward your purpose.

> Remember . . .
> Your purpose is one.
> Your callings could be several.
> Your assignments are many.

The only way to know whether or not you are called to do something is to act on your inner yearnings. Sometimes, a yearning (even if it seems random or unexpected) is a catalyst for something else that will be revealed along the way. As you step into your creativity, trust that something beneficial can always come from your efforts. Every endeavor you are *inspired* to launch into—even if you don't understand why—is an indicator of what you are here to accomplish. Movement isn't always linear. Life moves in different directions, so it is imperative that you remain flexible in how you think and how you approach your life. As you continue to move courageously, your life's purpose will be revealed. This process is all part of you creating your life.

It's important to understand that this yearning is hidden deeply within us for protection. While this may make it difficult for you to find, it also protects it from outside influences that can distract you, discourage you, or otherwise lead you astray. The very process of searching for it is a quest that helps you grow—another lesson on the path of creating the life you came here to have.

As you continue reading *Qreative Evolution*, you will discover guidance to help you find your purpose and calling. That feeling of yearning is your navigator. It is the gauge that guides you to what you are here to do. It draws you toward the sacred elements that construct your entire life. I call this "Qreative Gravity." You are being guided or "pulled" in the direction of your creative fulfillment as you learn to follow your heart. You are the ultimate creator of your life and your inner yearnings act as a type of GPS to lead you toward your success.

FINDING YOUR CREATIVE ANCHOR

Many people feel inspired to explore gifts in more than one creative area. What should you do if you feel inspired to explore multiple interests? Many people feel that if they want to explore several areas, they are being indecisive or are committing a form of self-sabotage by scattering their attention and "spreading themselves too thin." While this can be true, it may also not be true for you. Being interested in more than one creative calling—from sewing to cooking to aquascaping—might be evidence that you are gifted with a larger purpose than you realize.

I once gave a lecture at King's College in the 1990s, when it was still housed in the Empire State Building in New York City. During the questions and answer session, a young man asked, "What do you do if you want to do many different things and can't decide which one to focus your life on?"

I was inspired by the spark in his eyes. Not wanting to give him a generic answer about staying focused, I asked him what things he wanted to pursue. He said that what he loved most of all was architecture, but could not become an architect because he struggled with math. He also loved writing and politics. Learning even that much about him enabled me to understand enough to give him some genuine guidance. I told him he didn't have to choose between them—there was a way he could combine them all into one creative pursuit. I suggested that he could *write* about the *political ramifications* of *architecture.* Though he had many creative influences, the main thread in his life was his enthusiasm for architecture. His love of politics and writing helped him create a career centered around writing about architectural policy. A theater critic or playwright or lighting designer may each have theater as their anchor. A veterinarian, zookeeper, and dog toy designer may all have a love of animals as their anchor.

Your creative interests are not an either/or situation. Seek the thread that unites all your interests. It is there within you. You need only discover it and allow yourself to be guided by it. When you don't see an obvious thread linking seemingly unrelated interests, take heart: The thread that links these things is *you.*

"I think what made [my career] work was I never allowed myself to get any further than nine [years old]. I've been nine since 1933 and I've been nine all my life. I was nine this morning with the room service waiter. I danced with him to the music and he's trying to pour me coffee. That wasn't me, [that was the nine-year-old in me]."

—JERRY LEWIS

AN EXAMPLE OF MY OWN ANCHOR

I realized that as much as I love to create visual artwork, I also love to write stories, play the piano, and compose my own music. The same college teacher who told me I would never get a job at

Sesame Street also told me I would never find a way to combine my drawings, writings, and music. He had been trying for years and couldn't figure out how to do it himself so, of course, if he couldn't figure it out, he was sure I certainly couldn't.

Thankfully, I ignored him.

I recognized that there was a thread moving throughout many of the songs I had already written. I discovered that these songs were a combined portrait of some of the neighborhood girls I had grown up with. Some of these girls went through serious hardships. Some became pregnant as teenagers and were sent away, which I never understood. Because I was in junior high school at the time, it was devastating to see this happen to girls who had made some poor decisions or got in serious trouble with the wrong "friends."

The terrible circumstances these young girls faced hit me harder than I realized. At the time, I thought I was writing love songs, but they turned out to be songs about learning to love oneself. I wrote a jazz-rock opera about an artistic girl who was drawing her way through her challenges on her way toward loving herself. I realized that the theme of self-love became the thread that held together my love of stories and music. My storytelling, my music, and my visual arts all came together in this expression of love for my friends as a combined portrait of all the girls I wanted to honor. This process showed me that my naysaying college teacher was wrong again. (As an aside, I have long forgiven this teacher because I now understand how the discouragements in his life could have caused his negativity. It took me some time to understand and to get past that discouragement. Fortunately, with healing can also come wisdom and compassion.) By following my own heart and discovering what was inside of me, I was able to follow the thread of my multiple inspirations.

After struggling with how to combine art—which was my anchor—with storytelling, piano playing, and composing, I discovered that *I* was the thread that connected them all.

This leads me to ask you, what do you believe your creative anchor is? Think about what your creative priority is. What do you care about the most? What are the other interests that you think aren't related to your anchor?

"Every block of stone has a statue inside it and it is the task of the sculptor to release it."

—MICHELANGELO

OF NEWBORNS AND NEW SKILLS

Think of a newborn baby. New to the world, it is in need of love, careful nurturing and patience. There is so much for it to learn and grow into. Our feeling of wonder at the sight of new babies brings with it the understanding that they haven't yet learned what they need to know to survive in this world. They don't know how to walk or talk or even hold their own heads up. But they will. Everything you do for that baby helps it grow stronger and smarter.

When you approach everything new in your life as if it were a newborn baby, you will be much more patient with yourself. Don't rush. Take time to understand new concepts, new skills, or new goals—anything new to you requires patient compassion toward anyone and anything involved.

Another way to consider this is that something new to you is raw material. Be it a relationship, a job, a hobby, or a friendship, avoid looking at this new thing as a sign that "you've got what you wanted" and can now sit back and "enjoy it." Instead, see this new raw material as Michelangelo saw a block of marble: A new-to-you opportunity that requires your attention, your commitment, your enthusiasm, and your curiosity in order to discover the lessons this opportunity has for you.

FEELINGS ARE INDICATORS, NOT MOTIVATORS

The pressures of life don't change you as much as they reveal you. Challenges reveal where you are—mentally and emotionally—in that moment. It's difficult to know who you are deep down until extreme pressure comes upon you. For instance, it's possible that someone who was very generous when they didn't have much "becomes" greedy and selfish when they hit the lottery. It's not really that they "became" greedy; they were already greedy but didn't have much. Once they received wealth, it *revealed* what was truly within them all along. But it is also possible that someone whom others consider selfish is the first to volunteer when someone needs a kidney. These are examples of the complexity that lies within us—we ourselves may not even know what is within us until extreme pressure or overwhelming circumstances appear.

The quest for improvement is within us all in one way or

another. But improvement doesn't always mean "repair." Seeking to become better isn't an indication of being "broken," even if one feels that way.

Our emotions are not motivators. They are indicators. They are there to help you see where you are at any given moment so you can adjust as needed. They are gauges that monitor your state of being and present you with an opportunity to make adjustments as you move through your life. As human beings we will, of course, react rather than respond on many occasions. Many people have been motivated by their emotions and have regretted the outcome for years. But there is a way to cultivate your understanding of emotions so they aren't dangerously loaded when things get out of hand. Remember that as human beings we are meant to feel deeply as a way of understanding ourselves and learning how to best respond to life's circumstances. The way to cultivate this understanding is to keep in mind that emotions are not meant to motivate you but just to let you know what state of mind you are in. They are your gauge to reveal your state to yourself and be aware of how what you're going through is affecting you.

"You are your own best friend or worst enemy . . . choose wisely."

—TIMOTHY PINA

THE FOUR ESTEEMS

The word "esteem" is a noun that means admiration or respect. It can also be a verb, meaning "to admire or respect." Add the word "self," and you have self-esteem, which is confidence in your own talents or worth. Many of us go through life with low levels of self-esteem. This lack of self-respect obviously determines how we feel about ourselves, as well as the opportunities we take, the people we interact with, the way we care for ourselves, and even whether or not we use our creative talents to their greatest extent. In this state, you become sorely distracted from your awareness of your calling, which is a vital element in managing your self-esteem. Your calling is part of how you define yourself.

Why we lack self-esteem can depend upon our own unique DNA, our upbringing, and even our childhood environment. For many people, encouragement was nonexistent during childhood. Others found support from one person, only to be sabotaged by another. Still, others experienced a pivotal esteem-sapping moment that lowered the way they thought about themselves. Regardless of what eroded our self-worth, I assure you that we can reset our self-esteem.

I believe there are several types of self-esteem, positive and negative. In *Qreative Evolution*, we will consider four of them. Take an honest, judgment-free look at these descriptions and see if you can identify where your current level of self-esteem is. Remember, exploring this is part of your guided self-education; it gives you the opportunity to understand something about yourself.

1. Excessive Self-Esteem: Here is a situation in which someone holds themselves too high in their own estimation, many times thinking themselves better than others. This frequently comes with wealth or a position of power, or both, and involves looking down at someone (anyone) in order to feel superior. Ultimately, excessive self-esteem is the ego out of control. It can be a learned outlook. Perhaps a person grew up being told

they were "better" or "more" than others. Or, it can be a by-product of weak or damaged self-worth, as in fear hiding behind the facade of bravado. When a person fears they have nothing to offer, it is often easier to tear others down by using criticism, put-downs, and general negativity, rather than join motivated individuals as they build their dream lives. I believe excessive self-esteem is like a state of walking death. These poor souls are to be pitied if they cannot be reached at their core.

2. Low Self-Esteem: When someone doesn't recognize their self-worth, it becomes easy to wrongly see other people as "better than." Many people feel that they do not deserve good things, or are inferior to others. Low self-esteem can be a by-product of a neglectful or difficult childhood, which may leave a person paralyzed with self-pity, incapable of contributing anything of real value. The strange thing about low self-esteem is that it, like overly high self-esteem, is the ego out of control. It still leads someone to obsess about themselves and center all their attention on their own existence. In this case, attention is directed toward how inconsequential they believe their life is. While some try to soften or disguise it with self-deprecating humor or a "humble" attitude, low self-esteem still reveals the inability to see one's own self-worth.

3. Warped Self-Esteem: This is a particularly dangerous type of self-esteem because it leads primarily to destructive behaviors that stem from desires for revenge. Rather than healthy achievement that fulfills oneself and contributes to society, warped self-esteem centers on

achievement as a kind of fuel used to empower oneself so a person may become (in their mind) "superior" to others. It is gaining high positions through concerted and obsessive efforts that appear to be genuine and even praiseworthy. In reality, however, the effort is fueled by a desire to "show them" and "get even." It is out-of-control behavior that becomes self-worship. I remember the villain in *Superman III* making this statement, "It is not enough that I win . . . everyone else must fail." This sentiment is very real for many who suffer from warped self-esteem. The biggest problem with this form of self-esteem is that it has tragically led to some of the worst examples of dehumanization and outright evil in all of human history. Two examples from history of individuals who convinced themselves of the "fact" of their superiority are Adolf Hitler and Idi Amin. Not everyone with a warped self-esteem goes to these extremes, however. Even "everyday" bullies fit within this category.

4. Healthy Self-Esteem: Also known as high self-esteem, healthy self-esteem allows you to use perspective, as you acknowledge your gifts, your growth, your potential, and your place as a member of the world's society. You realize that like others, you are a valuable world citizen who always has room for growth. This growth escalates into evolution through deep, intimate self-exploration, self-study, and most of all self-love. This is the type of self-esteem whereupon you build your strengths, challenge your weaknesses, and learn from both. You know that you are evolving through a process that requires

every part of yourself to be accessed, exercised, and re-spected in the context of who you are and what you are called to do in life. You realize that where you are right now is valid and necessary and that you are capa-ble of genuine contributions wherever you are at any given moment. Individuals who are engaged in one of the previous self-esteems might regard someone with healthy self-esteem as arrogant. This is usually a help-ful gauge in determining the success of your efforts to embrace your healthy self-esteem. I find that when neg-ative people criticize you, it is a sign of progress. We thrive and invest in ourselves while supporting others who are seeking healthy self-esteem in the same way. This may sound idealistic, and it is, in the true spirit of the word.

YOU ARE NOT FLAWED

I truly believe that no one is flawed. This is among the most potent and life-affirming discoveries revealed to me on my jour-ney through *Qreative Evolution*.

However, many people think of flaws as our past personal failures, failures that came about because we are no good or lack the skill or intelligence or gifts necessary to succeed. Some people go as far as thinking they are irreparably broken or "of no use." *Merriam-Webster Dictionary* defines a flaw as "an im-perfection or weakness and especially one that detracts from the whole or hinders effectiveness."

What all these beliefs have in common is they leave people feeling like they don't have what it takes to accomplish their dreams and goals, and that their very existence is of no real value.

However, I have discovered through my own *Qreative Evolution* that it is impossible for a person to be flawed.

A clock can be flawed if it stops working. A car can be flawed after it has broken down to the point where it cannot run anymore. A termite-infested house can be flawed because the weakened wood means it is dangerous to live in.

But those are things. Things wear out. They begin to degrade the moment they are made. Many people think of themselves the same way they think of things: degrading over time, breaking down. But you are not a thing. You are a human being. And being such, you are a work in progress for the entire length of your life.

From the moment you were born, you began the journey of life as an "experiment" or a work in progress. You learn about yourself every day, throughout the entirety of your life. Depending upon how much you've learned, you can reap the benefits of attentive self-care or deal with the consequences of neglecting yourself. So many people think it's one or the other in this case. Nothing could be further from the truth.

When trouble reveals something negative in you, that negativity is not meant for you to judge yourself by. When you are ready for development or need to pay special attention in a specific area in your life, you start to recognize "problem areas." Many people incorrectly call these flaws. But in reality, shortcomings, challenges, and even illnesses all fall under the category of "assignments." This is a good place to think back on past and present challenges that you may have considered flaws. How do they make you feel? Consider reframing what you consider a flaw as an assignment.

I believe that when it's time to grow, you will receive an

assignment that will show you what you need to work on. When you are presented with one of these assignments, it is tempting to deny the lesson and instead throw up your hands and judge yourself as being flawed. As terrible as it may feel, calling yourself flawed is taking the easy way out. It is insulting yourself instead of recognizing and accepting the assignment that has been revealed to you for your improvement.

Here's another way to think about it: It's not a flaw; it's your next assignment, the next area you are being called to work on within yourself. Some assignments will be tremendously challenging and some will be basic, but—because so many of us resist change of any kind—we cling to old habits, such as calling ourselves flawed.

This is a form of denial. The revealed assignment is pointing you in the very direction of your progress, your personal promotion on your journey toward development. But because we have been brainwashed to be self-deprecating and inordinately self-critical, when an assignment shows up to help us grow, we label it a "flaw" and deny it, avoid it, or, even worse, completely ignore it.

WE ARE NOT FLAWED BECAUSE
WE ARE NOT FINISHED

Being a perpetual, lifelong work in progress means that you never "land." You never "arrive." You are always moving—sometimes sideways, sometimes backward, sometimes forward—and growing, constantly developing, and ever evolving.

As a human being, even when something breaks (your leg, your arm, or even your heart), it is not repaired. Instead, it heals. This is part of the perpetual evolution and cultivation from the inside out that is possible when you look at yourself as a work in progress.

"Don't fear mistakes; there aren't any."
—MILES DAVIS

NO ONE ELSE IS FLAWED EITHER

You are not flawed. Neither is anyone else. Everyone is in the process of refinement. We are all in on the journey of cultivating our lives. When we discover an area that needs attention, it means we are being shown our next level of growth. Again, that is *not* a flaw. It's an assignment, our next target to focus on.

Individuals who deny or ignore their assignments are difficult to be around. The benefits of the work they are being called to do are lost and, many times, they attempt to ease the pain and guilt of not taking care of themselves through meanness, obnoxiousness, or destructive activities.

Again, we are works in progress for our entire lives. Day in and day out, we move (hopefully) forward, learning and exploring. I hope this news removes the weight of "perfection" from anyone who thinks he has to perform "perfectly" without making a "mistake." This is a good time to remember what Miles Davis said. "Don't fear mistakes; there aren't any."

CHAPTER TWO GUIDED SELF-EDUCATION INQUIRY: YOUR EVOLUTIONARY WISDOM

Answering the questions at the end of each chapter is part of your *Qreative Evolution*. These questions—part of your self-designed curriculum—should not lead you to condemn or judge yourself. They are designed to illuminate what you need to be aware of.

Give life your full attention and your self-education will evolve into genuine growth.

Go get a pen and paper and get ready to honestly look at yourself. As you answer the following questions, remember that you are not flawed but a lifelong work in progress:

1. What is your life trying to communicate to you? Is it calling to you or is it screaming at you?

2. What are the three key challenges in your life right now? What do you believe they are revealing to you about your life's purpose?

3. What do you truly feel about humanity? How do your feelings reflect how you feel about yourself?

4. If you could do any kind of work, what would you find the most fulfilling?

5. Where do you feel you fall within the Four Self-Esteems?

Chapter Three
EVOLUTIONARY KNOWLEDGE

The more you discover about yourself, the more opportunities appear for you, and the more your life grows in the direction of your dreams. Evolutionary Knowledge inspires you to use one of the most valuable commodities you have—your time—to grow your knowledge. It's important to reserve regular time—daily if you can—to gain knowledge specific to your purpose and calling, then trust that knowledge enough to use it in your daily life. This is self-education in its best sense. Even when challenged by yourself or outside sources, the knowledge you have amassed is part of you. It acts as a gauge to guide your decisions and your actions. The following is an example of how the knowledge I had received through personal experience helped me stand my ground creatively.

DESIGNING A VERY SPECIAL MUPPET

As the creative director of character design at Sesame Workshop, my primary focus is the classic *Sesame Street* Muppets. I make sure some of the most famous and beloved characters in the world are represented properly. Whenever there is a new initiative based on a specific need, Sesame Workshop goes into research mode. Depending upon the initiative itself and what is needed to convey its message, either a classic *Sesame Street* Muppet character is designated for it or a brand-new Muppet is designed. Designing these new Muppets is also my responsibility.

One workday morning, I was approached by Dr. Jeanette Betancourt, the person in charge of Sesame Workshop's Autism Initiative. She told me that the team had decided that a brand-new *Sesame Street* character was needed for this initiative, and that this character would be on the autism spectrum. This character would not appear on the show itself, but would instead be featured in an illustrated book alongside two established Sesame characters, Elmo and Abby Cadabby. I was astounded at the serendipitous opportunity that was being presented to me as I had been working with children on the spectrum at the Eden II School on Staten Island in New York. No one at Sesame Workshop knew about this except Rachel Lunden-Carter, an intern at the Workshop, who had invited me to volunteer.

The experience was rewarding and challenging at the same time. Thanks to Rachel, I was able to work with these beautiful children at the school, in their homes, and on certain outings. It was deeply fulfilling. I saw difficulties and sometimes tremendous hardships. I witnessed how families did all they could to support their children who were on the spectrum. There were also, however, many beautiful moments that I will treasure for the rest of my life.

One such moment occurred on my last volunteer day. The girl I was assigned to work with was a joy; she completely stole my heart. Though she was nonverbal, she communicated through facial expressions and physical gestures. One day while playing with her, I held onto a puzzle piece a little too long. Growing restless, she gave me an expression of impatience as she took the piece out of my hand. Seemingly worried that I was offended (which, of course, I wasn't), she comforted me.

Part of the students' schooling included work skills, such as stuffing envelopes or assembling pens. Toward the end of my visit, the children went outside to the work skills trailers. I was asked to stand at the main entrance of the school as the children exited. As I stood outside at the doorway, the girl I had been working with passed by. After a few steps, however, she turned to look at me. Then she did something that chokes me up to this day: She walked over, took my hand, and began leading me to the trailers. She seemed to think that I was lost and didn't know where to go, and she wanted to help me.

This little girl touched me even before this act of kindness. But after she helped me "find my way," my heart was filled in a way that I knew would influence both my life and the work I did for *Sesame Street*.

When Dr. Betancourt approached me about designing the first autistic *Sesame Street* character, I realized why this special opportunity had come to me.

As a result, Julia the Muppet was born and appeared as a character in the book, *We're Amazing, 123*. She was received with open arms and tremendous gratitude, both in the autism communities and in the general population. She became so popular that the vice president of creative at Sesame Workshop decided that Julia should move beyond being an illustrated character in a book and become a physical Muppet on *Sesame Street*.

To be perfectly honest, I was against this. How could we possibly represent all the people on the autism spectrum with just one character? But one of the researchers at Sesame Workshop explained to me that we were not representing autism, but *pointing* to it and bringing it the attention it deserved. That made perfect sense to me. I got right to work on the designs for Julia, the *Sesame Street* Muppet.

Character design is storytelling at its core. I wanted to give the Julia Muppet special traits to show she was different. Not strange or odd, just different. The illustrated version of Julia already had an unusual angle to her eyes that helped show how focused she could be when engaged in something she was doing, such as drawing and painting, two of her favorite activities. I also wanted to do something subliminal with her nose. I enhanced the diamond shape I gave her in the illustrated version because I saw the children on the spectrum as "diamonds in the rough." Master Muppet builder, Rollin Krewson, told me I was asking her to do things with Julia that had never been done before at the Jim Henson Company, where they build and maintain all of the Sesame Street Muppets. I expressed to her that since we had never created an autism Muppet, this was the perfect opportunity to do things never before done in the Muppet world. She was extremely supportive and helped to fulfill my vision of Julia as a Muppet.

There was one trait, however, that was rejected by the *Sesame Street* executive producer at the time. Usually, when a Muppet or a human character would open an episode, he or she would look at the viewers and say some version of, "Oh, hi. Welcome to *Sesame Street*." This show-opening greeting is a tradition on the show. But as a child with autism, Julia was never going to address the viewers this way. In fact, whenever Julia appeared, she wouldn't engage with the viewers. Instead, she would be drawing or painting or playing with her stuffed rabbit, Fluffster.

To keep viewers from feeling put off by this lack of direct engagement, I felt I needed to give Julia a trait that would help the audience feel warmly toward her.

If Julia had human-like hair, I thought, it would make her look more like a human little girl. This would make her immediately appealing and relatable to viewers without her having to give the usual *Sesame Street* greeting. But our executive producer at that time did not like that idea and insisted that Julia's hair be fashioned from traditional Muppet materials, such as yarn, ostrich feathers, or some other hair-like material. This "hair debate" went on for a while. Because it was the executive producer making the decision, I didn't have much hope for giving Julia the one trait I believed would make a huge difference in how she was accepted. I understood the executive producer's thinking, but, as a character designer, I knew something different was needed.

That's when Dr. Jeanette Betancourt spoke up. She felt that maybe we should try things my way. And so Julia was built with bright orange human-textured hair. And it worked perfectly. When Julia made her *Sesame Street* debut as a Muppet, she was gazing down at her paper and drawing. Yet she looked so sweet that it felt as if a living girl was there on the screen. Julia was immediately welcomed and widely accepted. I am so grateful to Dr. Betancourt for giving the story behind the character design a chance to live.

THE POWER OF BEING SELF-TAUGHT

While there are courses that teach character design, in truth, they are really teaching character art. There is a tremendous difference between the two. Character *art* is drawing an already-established character or giving a new character a look and a pose. Character *design* is creating a believable entity that can convincingly deliver the content it is designed for. Both involve a hefty dose of self-education that might include watching endless hours of cartoons, puppet shows, and shows like *Sesame Street starting early in childhood in my case.* Character designers, however, fall in love with the way characters are used to move a story forward. In addition to analyzing a character's physical traits, they also evaluate personality, morals, quirks—anything that influences a character's behavior. Ultimately, the best character designers are writers who create entities with words rather than images in order to leave the visuals to the reader to imagine in their minds. But in all cases, character design, visual or otherwise, is done by storytellers. I am sharing this with you because storytelling is related to self-education.

> I realized that my childhood experiences informed the adulthood I would grow into. You have those experiences, too, in your past, based on your own individual journey. You may not have watched *Looney Tunes* like I did, which led to my love for character design, but there was something in your childhood that set you up for where you are now. Excavate through your history to extract those hints. These are the clues that can help guide you in your creative education.

This evolutionary approach to education translates to all types of creative endeavors, from cooking to classical music to car design. By immersing yourself in something you love, studying it deeply, and playfully exploring what you learn, you can create an evolutionary, self-designed education while perhaps simultaneously creating something of great value for yourself and others.

BUILDING YOUR OWN CURRICULUM

In Chapter One of *Qreative Evolution,* we briefly touched on the importance of creating your own curriculum. Let's delve deeper into what that means and how to approach it from the point of view of your personal *Qreative Evolution.*

An excellent and helpful tool I have discovered is a self-designed curriculum, which is a definite and growing course of study based on what you learn about yourself. A curriculum that changes and grows as you progress. In order for you to build your own most effective personal syllabus, you have to rely on your inner self. Letting someone else tell you what to study would be robbing you of the self-awareness you'll develop. Exploring who you are benefits you by introducing you to yourself. Knowing yourself well helps you understand, embrace, and *own* every aspect of your *Qreative Evolution.*

There is a way we can collaborate on your personal *Qreative Evolution.* There is an art to this kind of collaboration, and it must be approached with *you* at the core. This is the reason I use personal stories to help explain the ideas I share in this book. Storytelling is one way that I collaborate with you; in sharing something that happened to me and what I learned from the experience, I am hoping you will relate to what I went through or learn from my challenges in an area you may not have traveled yet. That said, there are events that you have experienced and lessons that you must learn that are exclusively yours. It is vital that you identify those, own them, and excavate them deeply to find the lessons earmarked just for you.

This cannot always be about what you do for and with others. I will say it again and again that you are creating your *own* life either on purpose or by accident. You will have to reference and research and study and practice on a whole new level in order to rise to the place your potential wants for you. You may find it challenging to concentrate on your own growth—especially in the face of other people's opinions and desires for you. Make the commitment to your studies and those concepts that require you to pay greater attention to your life. In time, this self-education will pay off. You will become a friend to yourself, which is essential toward making the best choices in life.

HOW TO CREATE YOUR OWN CURRICULUM

Get ready to examine yourself in a profound way. Go somewhere comfortable at your favorite time of the day and your favorite day of the week. Schedule a time for self-care when you can deeply focus on yourself at your own pace, without distractions or stressors. Think of the things you truly desire in your life and things you've always wanted to do. This is not the time to be practical, or to hold back. This is the time to delve deeply into your dreams and the purpose of your life. If those aren't clear to you right now, they will be soon. Show up for yourself regularly and search your heart for what deeply appeals to you. When your life is done, what do you want to have experienced? What do you want to have learned? What do you want to have accomplished? What do you want to have left behind as your legacy? Grab a notebook and a pen and list your desires. Fill a page if that's how you are led. Fill two, if you can. You will eventually narrow your self-designed curriculum focus to seven subjects, but for now, dig deep into what you want for yourself and make a list.

You may have this list after one sitting. Or perhaps it may take two or three meetings with yourself. Once you have your list, choose seven subjects to focus on. I say seven, to help you align with the seven Qreative areas of life outlined earlier and because I find that anything more than this can be overwhelming. If you are struggling to choose, close your eyes and think about what you want for yourself. You will find certain desires have a stronger pull on your attention than others. Write down seven of these. Then explore the steps that you can make in the direction of those desires. Is there a local organization dedicated to your dream? What books can you read to help you? Are there any online courses you could take or videos to explore? Do you know someone doing what you'd like to do? We are fortunate we live in the era of online search engines, which can help identify resources that will support us as we explore our desires. I am being deliberately vague here because this is a very intimate and personal process of discovery, but I will tell you this, map out your next steps (read a book, talk to a person, visit a place, etc.) so that you can get started on your personal curriculum.

How freely are you willing to dream? Dig into your desires with enthusiasm. Make your notes and see where they will take you. Trust me. My dreams have always been very big (although small dreams are good, too). Even when I didn't believe at all that most of them were possible (and there were plenty of people to help me feel that way), I still managed to write down my dreams. It was fun to think of what it would be like to be an artist for the Muppets, or to meet and work for a famous comic book artist, or to go to the Galapagos Islands someday.

In the case of the Galapagos Islands, I had dreamed of going there my entire adult life. Seeing the pictures and videos of this extraordinary and unique place convinced me that it would help me grow as an artist and a human being. One afternoon, the then-CEO of National Geographic's Lindblad Expeditions, Dolf Berle, called. He had noticed some of the writing and presentations I had done for the Norman Rockwell Museum, where he is also chairman of the board. He had had an idea of starting an artist-in-residency program and asked if I would consider going on a ten-day expedition with him . . . to the Galapagos Islands!

I had collected clippings, videos, and photographs from others who had gone there, and I was determined to go there some day. And here it came, not only as a gift, but as a paid assignment during which I would be treated as part of the crew with all the additional access and perks.

Another dream came true and all I had done was actively believe in it. Collecting pictures and videos tapped me into the benevolence of belief, which manifested one of the greatest trips of my life.

Today, I live in perpetual gratitude when I think about how many of my dreams are coming true. In fact, many of my dreams have been fulfilled in ways that far surpassed even my wildest imagination.

How about you? What dreams do you have for your future? You may be tempted to skip this step, but I encourage you to stay with it and stay with your dreams. Writing them down is a step toward igniting their manifestation.

When I was young, writing out my dreams was just a game that I played. I had no idea how much power there was in committing my desires to paper, then living them over and over in my imagination. I would often read through my "dream notebook" to pacify myself when I was feeling particularly down. I quickly learned that my dream-listing was a way to plant seeds. Because I kept my dreams constantly in my attention, I moved almost subconsciously toward them all.

I believe that this book, *Qreative Evolution*, can help you develop your courage and commitment to your dreams.

MY LIBRARY OF LITERARY "FRIENDS"

It is vital that you feed your mind, just as you feed your body, with nutritious food. But what is food for the mind? It is material that inspires you, gives you hope, educates you, and leaves you with an inner buoyancy. We do grow weary or sad sometimes. Feeling low or uninspired is a natural occurrence when you don't take deliberate actions to fend off negative feelings. Having a "Library of Friends" can help with those feelings.

Books can become mentors in your life. They are the thoughts of living individuals who are either still with us but hard to connect with in person, or who have left their thoughts for us. This is why I call them friends. When humans share their thinking with others, the results can be profound, both positively and negatively, which means it is important to be deliberate about the books you read.

I want to share twelve of the most important books that comprise what I call "My Library of Friends." I think of these books as anchors that ground me and help me recharge. They educate me and inspire me so I can be my best self. I decided to stop at these twelve titles because I noticed I always learn more each time I reread these books. Sharing my own favorite books is my approach to helping you with your own search. So, please compose your own list of titles to include in your own "Library of Friends."

"You don't have to burn books to destroy a culture. Just get people to stop reading them."
—RAY BRADBURY

These books were not *chosen* as friends as much as they were *discovered* to be friends as I read them. Just like you cannot choose who will become a great friend until you have discovered a kindred spirit. Seek books that speak to you the most. Then add them to your "Library of Friends." Move on to other books, adding to your library those that resonate the most with the vision and direction of your life. It can take a lifetime to find the books—a.k.a. "friends"—that are genuinely yours but it is worth it. There are many books that speak to me but these twelve speak what I needed to hear the most:

Toward a Meaningful Life by Rabbi Simon Jacobson: I use this book as a companion to the Bible. It is a remarkable collection based on the astounding teachings of Rabbi Menachem Mendel Schneerson, and an examination of the depth, beauty, and purpose of humanity.

Strength to Love by Dr. Martin Luther King Jr.: This is among the most powerful books I have ever read. I recommend getting the unabridged version, which includes a chapter based on my favorite sermon by Dr. King, "The Three Dimensions of a Complete Life." The title speaks for itself.

Principle-Centered Leadership by Stephen Covey: I learned the important difference between principles and values from this book. I also gained a deep understanding of what integrity is and how it shapes our lives.

Free Play by Stephen Nachmanovitch: I was inspired by this book's thoughtful consideration of creativity's evolutionary aspect.

Mastery by George Leonard: This is the single most power-ful book I have read on how (and why) habits can have such a grip on people, as well as how to break their hold on us so we can live in a more intentional way.

The Art Spirit by Robert Henri: This book reveals the deep importance of creative self-education for artists of all types, giving the reader a realization of the life-shaping power of creativity.

The Courage to Teach by Parker Palmer: When I read this book, I felt so aligned with it that it seemed as if I had written it myself. However, it took thoughts and ideas I have about ed-ucation and teaching so much further and taught me so much about concepts I didn't know how to articulate for myself.

A Different Kind of Teacher by John Taylor Gatto: A vital look at the relationship between confidence and the intentional contributions we make in life. At the heart of the book is the belief that empty praise has no value in helping anyone, espe-cially children, with their self-esteem.

Technopoly by Neil Postman: A powerful exposé and severe warning about the abuse of and over-dependence on technol-ogy. Though it was first published in 1996, the book has taken on a new relevance in today's age of smartphones and artificial intelligence.

The Craftsman by Richard Sennett: A detailed and relatable history that lays out the value of technology while illustrating how the natural processes of humanity are in desperate need of restoration.

Danson: The Extraordinary Discovery of an Autistic Child's Innermost Thoughts and Feelings by Michele Pierce Burns and Danson Mandela Wambua: As we follow young Danson's brilliant work, we are given proof that children are among our most gifted teachers.

Pour Your Heart into It by Howard Schultz: I have read many books on business. This one—the story behind the Starbucks coffee shops—is one of the few that really does reveal the heart of a businessman who puts people before commerce. Schultz shows how business can be conducted with genuine integrity and how one's history, even if laden with hardships, can positively impact what they do in life.

"I have never let my schooling interfere with my education."

—MARK TWAIN

YOUR SUPPORT DIARY
(A.K.A. YOUR JOURNALNOTEBOOK)

There is another addition to my "Library of Friends" that is in a class by itself: my journal. It's a "self-portrait," a personal resource that I use as an ever-evolving guide. It is a record of my understandings and a collection of the wisdom of others that inspires and directs me. I refer back to my journal regularly. I encourage you to do the same.

MY FOUNDATIONAL BOOK

You may find that you have one foundational book in your life that you return to consistently. My life revolves around spirituality. This is why

the foundational book of my life is the Bible. It
influences what books I bring into my library,
so I consider the Bible to be in a category all its
own. I have many translations of it, as well.
Some are the more modern versions, while
others are older versions in a language closer
to the original writings.

HOW I "BEFRIEND" MY BOOKS

I don't just read my books; I *consume* them. I underline phrases that spark thought. I add sticky notes to pages I want to reference again and again. I write notes in the margins. I draw boxes around paragraphs I want to emphasize. If a book has wisdom to share, I highlight it and add—in my own words—what I've learned. Here is an example of how I make a book my own. The book is my copy of *Toward a Meaningful Life*.

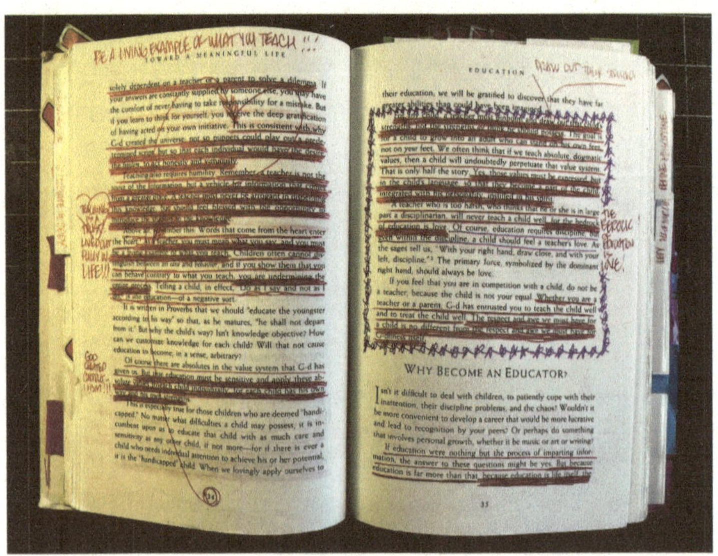

"What happens if you lose that book with all those notes and highlights and stickies in it?" people ask me.

My answer is simple. When I devour books like this, they become part of me. This level of immersion helps me to "own" the content, absorbing it into my mind and heart. Even when I don't carry the book with me, I always have its wisdom in me.

My relationship with this particular book grew even deeper when I reached out to the author, Rabbi Simon Jacobson, for permission to use the above picture. When I described what his book means to me and how I approached it with my notes and stickies, he was intrigued and wanted to meet me. We spent an afternoon together and began a personal friendship beyond the book.

"You are your best teacher, so be your best student."
—LOUIS HENRY MITCHELL

GUIDED SELF-EDUCATION

There are reasons why you come to any particular interest. You may not know those reasons, but they are your own. Whatever education you engage in should also be your own, meaning that the courses you discover to take and the books revealed for you to read and the mentors you are led to seek out and the activities you engage in as you learn more about your interests, should all be embraced by you.

You will have a deeper commitment to the subject when you commit to your own educational path. Don't let anyone work everything out for you. Working it out yourself is not always an easy task but the extra effort is worth it. Education comes from personal experience, not from "mentors" who want to give you too much information on any given subject. The best teachers will introduce a topic to you, then step back so you can investigate it yourself. It's essential that you uncover your own resources, learn what you think is important, try things out, course adjust, and continue growing. This is how a skill or a topic becomes yours. And only then will the act of educating yourself help you evolve into the person you are meant to become. Again, good teachers will give you room to approach any subject from your own angle. They are supportive guides who expect you to find—and follow— your own educational path. In Chapter Five, we will explore the *Qreative Evolution* approach to the value and impact of mentors. They can help teach you things without you ever having to meet them. But the lessons can be as potent as if you had.

LISTEN, YOU ARE BEING CALLED

While there is courage in admitting that you have a desire, it takes even greater courage to educate yourself in all facets of that desire. You have obligations in your life. You may have work and family obligations. Perhaps you serve in your community or house of worship. There are many tasks competing for your time. There are people who may try to talk you out of what you want. I know how easy it is to ignore the call of a desire— and how easy it is to talk yourself out of exploring that desire. What I say to you is, please do not push it aside. It is a part of you, and it is actually your heart communicating with you. The very act of engaging in your desire, educating yourself about it, and sharing it, shapes who you become. Your desire influences the direction you go, the people who enter your life, the opportunities that appear before you, and how you think, act, and see the world. Not only does your desire help make you who you are, it creates your life.

"Self-education is, I firmly believe, the only kind of education there is."

—ISAAC ASIMOV

NOT SURVIVE, BUT THRIVE

The way you think about anything in your life can make a tremendous difference in how you think and feel about yourself. It can even impact the level of energy you approach people and situations with. Where survival is a form of desperation, thriving is the enjoyment of inspiration and celebration.

Survival most definitely has its place, but it should not be the norm for any of us. We are here for greater things than merely surviving. We are here to thrive. While there are medical, financial, family, and other situations that may make day-to-day life challenging, many people who find themselves "just surviving" have arrived at this place because of their own choices. Allowing judgment, bitterness, anger, resentment—anything that can darken or numb your minds and hearts—will only destroy your potential. Settling for "average" will not help you create the life you are meant to live. You may think you are protecting yourself from the judgment of others, or the sweat of effort, or the sting of "failure" by doing less for yourself. In reality, you've fallen victim to the "epidemic of average" by ignoring your dreams and refusing to grow.

Life, when lived well, is a process of perpetual growth. When I say that you are a work in progress, I mean that no one should stay the same. In fact, you can't. You change as you age and you have the power to influence the direction and quality of that change. You will be a different person at the end of your life than you were in the middle or at the beginning of it. As you travel forward, your perspective on life can help you remain true to your gifts or abandon them if you aren't living with intent. To help you develop your perspective, I offer you this series of paradigm shifts. They can help reframe the fixed beliefs so many of us were taught from childhood.

NOT BALANCE, BUT HARMONY

In an orchestra, all musical instruments are played in whatever order the music indicates. There are specific notes, a certain volume, a speed, a mood, and more, all assigned by the composer who wrote the music. There is also a conductor, who oversees how the music is being played and guides the large group of musicians—each playing a different instrument—as they work together to create a musical experience.

If each instrument was balanced with each other and did the same thing, at the same volume, at the same time, the result would not be music, but noise. Everyone doing everything at the same time is chaos.

For a first-hand example of what I am talking about, I invite you to find an online recording of an orchestra performing Beethoven's Ninth Symphony. As you watch and listen, you'll notice subtleties that would be missed if all of the instruments, from the timpani drums to the violins, were evenly balanced, playing all at their individual top volume. The drums would easily cancel out the violins, and the brass would overshadow the woodwinds. If all instruments were played in absolute balance, the musical inflections that speak to the listener's heart would be lost in the monotony of sound. It would be impossible to experience the piece's drama, emotions, and subtleties if balance were the composer's priority.

Another musical example is "Let It Be," by the Beatles. The song starts with a beautiful piano passage. But if it didn't lower in volume before Paul McCartney begins to sing, we wouldn't have the opportunity to hear the beautiful, almost whispered, lyrics. There is a place for the piano to be the focus, and there is a place for it to drop back to a supporting role so the voice can be the focus of the song.

There is a lot of talk about living a balanced life, but just as with an orchestra, if you were to attend to each of the things in your life with equal time and equal energy, you would be exhausted. It is okay to be most enthusiastic about specific parts of your life, and it is okay to spend more time on your desires than you do, say, on listening to your neighbor complain about something or doing laundry. The art of life requires the artist to select what is emphasized, what is de-emphasized, and what kind of attention each element in a composition is given. You are an artist and you can do the same.

THE POWER OF IMBALANCE

There are things you don't want to give much attention to, while there are other things you'd like to focus on. Balance is not the desired result:

- Health: You do not want to balance sickness with health.
- Wealth: You do not want to balance poverty with wealth.
- Knowledge: You do not want to balance ignorance with knowledge.
- Peace: You do not want to balance stress with peace.
- Joy: You do not want to balance sadness with joy.
- Honesty: You do not want to balance deception with honesty.
- Love: You do not want to balance hatred with love.

Therefore, just as in music, I invite you to reconsider the idea of balance in every area of your life. What you should look for is a complete and total *imbalance*—in your favor—of the good things in life, the things you are enthusiastic about. You want to invest so much on your own progress and potential that the scales of life are tipped toward growth. You want an abundance of favor on your side. If you balance your unhealthy activities (sitting hours at your desk, eating poorly) to your healthy activities (taking a daily walk, getting enough sleep), the unhealthy activities would "drown out" any benefits the healthy activities could give you. If you spent your money in the same ratio as you saved it, you would never establish a rainy day fund. This example holds true with every area of your life.

When it comes to the positive things in life, you want a favorable *imbalance* on your side. This is actually *harmonizing* your life. You want as little of the things that take away from your best life as possible. You want more positive, and less negative. As with the musical examples, harmonizing the instruments with each other will highlight and emphasize their best use.

Personally, I do not want a glass that is half full *or* half empty. I want a glass that is overflowing with the best life has to offer so there is more than enough to enjoy and share. The only time I want an empty glass is when it comes to anything negative that can steal the best of what life can truly be. Unfortunately, there is no such empty glass. We will all have to deal with setbacks, shortcomings, and obstacles. But, when you work toward harmonizing them, you will learn how to minimize the detriments and maximize the benefits.

How can you "tip the scales in your favor"? For so many, the scales are tipped the wrong way, creating a life that is challenging and bleak. This can be an individual's own doing, perhaps because they have a negative outlook or won't engage in activities that uplift and educate. But difficulty can also come from listening to the wrong people. Someone else may have decided that all life (or just your life) is hard and dreams never come true. It is not always easy to do, but please practice ignoring this type of negativity. It is harmful to your success and your entire life. If you focus on what is important in your own life, what is absolutely essential in coming into the fullness of your potential, you will see that life's scales should always favor you.

As you continue on, remove as much negativity from your life as possible. The best way to do this is to focus on getting what's right on your side, such as surrounding yourself with dreamers and doers. Bring as many "right people" as you can with you. It is essential that you associate with positive, conscientious, supportive people who will help tip the scale of favor to your side. These are your true family members. This is your tribe.

As important as supportive people are to your development and happiness, it's important to spend regular time alone. Not with the television on or music playing or a podcast running. Alone in silence. Creating your self-education curriculum requires that you discover what you need to do and where you need to go. Developing this deep self-awareness requires silence and a notebook. You are establishing a deeply intimate relationship with yourself. This cannot be done with distraction.

Being alone in stillness can be very uncomfortable for some people. I would remind those individuals to practice it anyway. It is a spiritual and evolutionary investment in your creativity and your life. It is in our DNA to have times of genuine and total quiet. Our ancestors had few options outside of silence; they were more in tune with their thoughtlives than we are in our loud, bright, distracting modern age. This time of reflection and self-discovery is vital. Fiercely protect this time.

NOT DISCIPLINE, BUT TRAINING

When you focus on training in ways that you enjoy, discipline comes easily. This is very much like confidence being the by-product of commitment. I'll give you an example: I need to participate in aerobic exercise to stay healthy, but I don't like to run. But I do love to use the rebounder, which is a small trampoline that gives me a great aerobic workout without the monotony and jarring impact of running. If running were my only workout option, I most likely would avoid exercise altogether. However, I don't have to force myself to use the rebounder. You don't *will* yourself to be disciplined. You access your natural discipline by discovering activities that fit your personality, preferences, and life. Think of the saying, "Enjoy the fruits of your labor." Your discipline manifests the "fruit" that grows when you cultivate purpose-driven habits that you enjoy. What do you believe are the purpose-driven habits that can enhance your life? When you write down your purpose-driven habits, you begin the process of committing to them. Is there a way you can easily fit these habits into your daily life?

NOT DOWNTIME, BUT DEVELOPMENT TIME

We must make time to rest and relax, for our wellness and our creativity. Instead of thinking of this dormant period as "downtime," think of rest as "development time." I realize it may sound as if I think we should always be "doing something." Actually, the opposite is true. I want you to see downtime not as a random, unplanned lazy period where you "veg out," but as an intentional pause you give yourself so that you can process information, as well as rest, review, and renew. Development time is deliberate and planned.

NOT REJECTION, BUT DIRECTION

In my experience, the people you should avoid will naturally be repelled by how you live your genuine life. Showing a commitment to your growth, having a positive mindset, believing in yourself, engaging in educational activities, and supporting others, will attract the people and opportunities that align with who you are becoming. So, when someone rejects you, see this as a gift. You are being protected from a negative influence, someone you shouldn't be involved with.

This frees you up to move in a positive direction so that you have room to continue pursuing who and what you are meant to be in your life. Rejection can hurt, but you can heal from its effects if you focus on your gifts and your purpose, and just keep going. Soon, you will find yourself in a higher and more successful place.

NOT LISTENING, BUT HEARING

When someone speaks or music plays or some other sound appears, are you able to listen for the message within it? Or do you just hear it in the background, if at all? This one is an age-old concern, but one that really needs to be addressed. When I was young, some of my schoolteachers would yell at us during class. I don't think any of us listened to what they were saying—we just heard noise. Later on, I actually started listening to them and what I heard were messages. Our teachers were trying to reach us. They were saying things like, "Don't you realize you are throwing your life away?" and, "You are looking for trouble in the future if you don't take this time in your life seriously." Even though I didn't believe those comments were aimed at me—especially in junior high school, when I started listening—I began to cultivate an awareness of how many of us were blowing our time as teenagers. Yes, we were kids and should have fun, but why not make it productive fun rather than getting involved in negative activities or doing nothing at all?

I began playing less touch football and more piano. Because I started listening and not just hearing, even the things I read had more meaning to me than before. A new level of self-access developed and I was truly on a new path in life.

When I got to high school and I discovered a special book by the famous illustrator, Norman Rockwell, I didn't just look at the pictures anymore. I started reading his words and the book came alive. Over time, I began "hearing" how those wonderful pieces of art came into existence. So listening with my ears helped me to listen with my mind, which led right to listening to my heart, which led to discovering what I was to do with my life.

NOT DESTINATION, BUT JOURNEY

You may have heard the saying, "It's all about the journey." As great as it is to reach your destination, the journey itself is much more rewarding, and certainly more educational. Destinations are end points. Journeys are processes of time, from one point toward another point. A journey is a bit like a dance. You move toward the end of a song, but, oh, how wonderful the dance is before you get to that final note and the dance is over. You don't usually think of having come to the end of the dance, but you do think of the moves that occurred during that dance. Even the missteps that were corrected along the way become part of the dance's story. When you come right down to it, the only real destination—at least here on Earth—is death. The grave marks the end of this journey as we know it. You are a work in progress for the entire journey of life until then. You don't arrive at your destination until it is all done.

This list of paradigm shifts can grow continuously and it would be worth investigating what concepts you can reexamine in light of the journey you are taking. More examples of these shifts include:

Not Busy, But Productive

Not Happiness, But Joy

Not Reactive, But Responsive

Not Achievement, But Fulfillment

Feel free to add more to this list!

NOT REINVENTING YOURSELF, BUT REDISCOVERING YOURSELF

Have you ever wished someone would give you a whole life makeover? So many of us get to a place of frustration or low productivity and feel like we need to reinvent ourselves in order to move forward in a successful way. As enticing as a do-over seems, let me ask you something: What happened to that person who was on fire before things went flat? What happened to the curious person who was committed to realizing their big dream? That person is still you.

I believe that reinventing oneself can be a form of self-abandonment. Who you were, who you are, and who you are becoming are the same person. You are "in the process" of living. You are a beautiful form of raw material that is ready to be discovered and designed into your most successful self.

Many of us feel like we've been detached from the child we once were. The child who was full of wonder and excitement and curiosity. That child is still part of you. Under all that "adult-ing" clutter is a beautiful champion of life who can show you the way back to who you really are.

Once you are able to *remember* who you are, you will have the knowledge needed to fine-tune the course you are on, or discover a new path. You can start fresh by reaching back to take the hand of that young mentor, who was the child you started life as. You will eventually discover that you aren't really reaching backward but forward. You were just facing the wrong way.

YOUR THOUGHTLIFE

I enjoy coming up with words and phrases that act as anchors to secure my thoughts and remind myself of a more evolutionary way of thinking. That's why, throughout *Qreative Evolution*, I have shared the words I often use. You may see these words as unusual. I enjoy assigning words redefinitions and using unusual wordsmithing to both get your attention and to help you see the uniqueness of the ideas and paradigm shifts I am sharing. Such words include "thoughtlife" (mentioned earlier) and "journalnotebook." Even the way I spell "Qreative" is intentional. I want to grab your attention and help you look deeper—"pay attention"—in ways you may not do otherwise. These unusual words ignite the imagination. For imagination is where the act of creating your life truly begins: in your thoughts. You live accomplishments in your thoughts before you live them externally.

One of these words refers to how you live in your thoughts. "Thoughtlife" reminds us to be aware of the stories running in our heads. Plant the seeds of positivity in your mind and guard against poisonous distractions that compromise who you are and what you were called here to do. One of our greatest human endowments is the ability to think deeply and with great imagination.

LIKE DREAMS, THOUGHTS ARE SEEDS, TOO

In nature, weeds can be easy to identify but difficult to eliminate entirely. Likewise, the roots of the thoughts we live with can run deep and long; thoughts we have today may have been planted during our infancy. Without even understanding the negative words, newborn babies can absorb the energy of the words spoken in their presence. Words do have power to them. There is a vibe and a life to them. The age-old saying, "Sticks and stones can break my bones, but words will never harm me," is among the greatest of all deceptions. Many have healed from broken bones, but so very many never find relief from the things they were told as children, or even as adults.

As with any "life assignment," there is always an opportunity to examine and extract the words that have cultivated pain in you. However, we do need to understand the power of words a bit more before digging into how to restore the joy.

"We suffer more often in imagination than in reality."
—SENECA

YOUR WORDLIFE

Your *wordlife* comprises the words you use to speak to yourself. They are the words you use to create your thoughts. Your wordlife can be a place where you learn to thrive, survive, or crash, depending upon how you speak in your own mind. Among our greatest vices is the negative language we use to communicate with ourselves. "That was *stupid* of me!" "I *can't* do that!" "I'll *never* achieve that goal!" When we use negative language with ourselves, we can risk thinking and even behaving negatively. When we use positive language such as "What if I try this and it actually works?" "I've tried new things before and many of them went well!" "If I don't try I'll never know if this can work!" we begin to empower ourselves toward the fulfillment of our calling.

This is especially true because of the bombardment of

negative news and information that surrounds us constantly, putting us at risk for absorbing negative messages. We live in our thoughts and the words that are allowed in can guarantee—positively or negatively—our life's results.

"Be always at war with your vices."
—BENJAMIN FRANKLIN

So many people short-circuit their lives' momentum with their own words. What we hear ourselves saying with our mouths influences the inner tone and mood within us, which is the place from where we create our lives. We "think" our results into being. Hearing anything repeatedly over time—aloud or in our heads—will affect our thinking. The pattern—joyful or despondent, hopeful or dismissive, or anything else—of your thinking is determined by the thoughtlife you live, which in turn is formed by the wordlife you speak. Moods, thoughts, and words are all intertwined, and work with each other to influence the choices you make.

I want to be absolutely sure that you understand that the words you use in your thoughts will seriously affect the outcome of your life. Your own voice, speaking the words you most often use, is what you hear in your mind. Your own voice influences you like no other voice. It is vital to remember that you are still creating your life even when the words you speak to yourself are negative. You will see the corresponding manifestations of the thoughtlife you live.

Use words that are in direct relationship with what you are seeking to accomplish. Never speak contrary to your daily success. If you need help finding and choosing positive, powerful, life-changing words, look to your personal Library of Friends and your collection of quotes; you will find great mentors there. My own purpose statement from Chapter One is among my most cherished affirmations.

ALARM WORDS

In your thoughtlife, you speak to yourself either intentionally or unconsciously. The more you feed on words and ideas that enlighten and encourage you, the more your thoughts will live in a mental environment of positive energy. With time, this type of positive thinking will happen automatically and un-consciously. There will be times, however, even with the most positive thinking, that you will generate thoughts that tell you something is wrong. You may have strayed off the path of your good progress, perhaps someone or something distracted you, or a situation might cause worry or some other anxiety. You may even be having an off day and your thoughtlife brings up words that define the fear and worry that appear in your thinking. I call these words "alarm words."

Alarm words are not meant to be embraced or accepted. Nor are they meant to be ignored. They are meant to make you aware of the state you are in mentally and emotion-ally. Remember, emotions are indicators, not motivators. They are very much like the smoke from a fire. The smell of smoke draws attention to the fire. First, you smell the smoke before you see the fire. If no one smells the smoke, a small fire can expand quickly into a raging inferno. You will have words that are your "smoke alarms." When you hear yourself saying words that reveal a state of negativity in you, you are being warned that you have somehow gotten off track and need to return to your positive place. This is not about obsessing over each and every word you say. It is about remaining aware of where you are at any given moment, and listening for any alarm words you are hearing in your head or aloud.

"As I began to love myself, I found that anguish and emotional suffering were only warning signs that I was living against my own truth."
—CHARLIE CHAPLIN

There are reasons why words like "failure" and "mistakes" cause us stress and anxiety. When an alarm word appears in your head or your conversation, take some time to explore it. What is this word revealing? Is there a specific area—relationship, professional, family, financial, somewhere else—where you might be struggling? An alarm word is a wake-up call of sorts. It grabs our attention and asks us to focus on the area where we need help. Searching and addressing this area is an assignment, designed to help you grow and become wiser.

WATCH WHAT YOU SAY

In your everyday conversations, avoid complaining, gossiping, fear-mongering, self-deprecation, lying, cursing, making fun of your failures or anyone else's, and negativity. Embracing words that generate thoughts of failure or mistakes is going against your best mindset. Use your precious time to think uplifting thoughts that will elevate you.

Everyone has his or her own set of alarm words. It is vital to identify what your alarm words are. Do you begin mentioning your fatigue when you are experiencing an unpleasant situation with a family member? Do you find yourself using specific curse words when something has made you angry? Do you tell people to leave you alone when you are overwhelmed at work? When you can identify the words that pop up in your vocabulary when you are facing negativity, you can use this knowledge to your advantage. The alarm words become tools—like the smoke alarm many of us have in our homes—to let you know that something is up. You may not immediately realize what is bothering you, but when you've identified your alarm words, you'll know that it's time to examine what is happening in your life.

LIFE WORDS

Cultivate what I call "life words." These are expansive words that give us joy and help us grow. Just as with alarm words, life words can be unique to you. Life words are positive words like learning, growing, searching, exploring, investigating, practicing, traveling, cultivating, discovering, playing. Recognize the words that give you joy and encouragement. Make a list of them. Write them where you will see them, on a whiteboard, sticky note, or in your journalnotebook. Life words will elevate your thinking and bring you back to your calling. You can use life words to jolt your progress, or at least use it as a "pattern interrupter" to disrupt old destructive thinking patterns and help accelerate your growth. In the section on alarm words, I deliberately left out examples of negative words because I didn't want this book to be a source of such things. I would rather guide you toward your best thinking. Speaking life words steers your thought patterns toward purpose-driven progress.

There is a movie entitled *Arrival* that mentions something called the Sapir-Whorf Hypothesis. This theory looks at how our speech influences our thought patterns. According to the theory, the words you speak directly influence the life you live. Although we don't know to what degree, we have certainly seen how our own self-talk influences our thought patterns. It's a form of recycling according to *Arrival*'s screenwriter of Eric Heisserer. In an interview about his screenplay, he said, "I believe that our language absolutely does inform our reality and shapes it. I do believe that the language that we constantly recycle in our own world absolutely shapes our reality and can become our prison."

Thoughts and words are both seeds. You must be deliberate about what you plant (think and say), and what you allow others to "plant" into the fertile soil of your mind. Your mind will grow whatever you allow to be planted in it.

WHAT ABOUT THE DARK SIDE OF OUR THOUGHTLIFE?

It would be irresponsible of me not to address the other side of our humanity, the side that we must all face, in ourselves and in others: The dark side of the human condition.

Star Wars taught us a very important lesson: "The dark side" is real. It is a place where anger and even hatred live. Things happen in this life that push and pull you every which way. Life is not always easy, nor is being a human in general. You have experienced things that have torn at your heart. I, too, have suffered through indescribable emotional agony. I learned right in the middle of it that if I submitted to my dark feelings, I could have completely lost myself. I knew that losing myself would be the death of my creativity, my fellowship with humanity and, ultimately, my relationship with myself.

Many people live under the weight of anger and bitterness. Some precious people harbor deeply ingrained feelings of hatred toward others. Some harbor hatred for themselves. For some reason, many extremely creative people can be self-destructive and even suicidal.

I have never felt suicidal but before gaining an understanding of what I am sharing in this book, I was bitter and angry at myself many times. I had a ferocious temper and was easily discouraged as a teenager. At one point during a particularly dark time in my life, I was ready to give up on becoming a professional artist. I was struggling with getting work. I was also a young father trying to understand what it meant to raise another human while simultaneously facing severe marital challenges. I found the challenges I faced to be almost too much to bear. I offered my art supplies to my best friend and decided to get any job I could just to survive and take care of my son.

But something happened.

It wasn't a dramatic flash of inspiration or encouragement from someone important or an unexpected act of reawakening. It was my deep creative yearnings speaking to me. During this period, I had stopped engaging with the creative activities that I loved, but my yearnings told me it was time to return to them. Music I had written was still faintly in the back of my mind. I hadn't played the piano for so very long. Drawings I had done and characters I had created were ghostly images in my distracted imagination. I decided to spend a little time each day writing, playing the piano, and drawing.

What happened was every time I spent a little time on any of the things I had loved (but had been too distracted to pursue), my creative "life force" grew. I felt peace and happiness and hope. I am a creative person. We all are. Creative pursuits center me and remind me of my purpose. Without them, it was easy to become overwhelmed by negativity and allow myself to sink further and deeper into darkness. Reintroducing positive creative activities to my life, even in small but daily doses, elevated my outlook and returned light into my life. I began to overcome the things that were keeping me from my true self and my true calling. I was "rediscovering" myself.

This experience reminded me that as a human, I have a dark side. I had to understand how real it was before I could move through it. An "assignment" was presented to help me magnify my self-awareness. I needed to acknowledge the

> darkness, to face it, but not embrace it or wallow
> in it. Understanding this was the only way to
> reconnect with my true self and my true purpose.
> Ignoring or denying our dark side makes it
> deceptively easy to unknowingly submit to it.

"In admitting my shadow side I learn who I am and what God's grace means."
—BRENNAN MANNING

I recommend that you take a long and deep look at your thoughtlife. Notice the dark places that can become encumbrances if you don't monitor and adjust them. Do not be ashamed when you discover things that can be destructive to yourself or others. Every individual has areas that hide in the shadows. When you realize that all humans have undesirable traits and quirks, you may feel less fear about actively searching out yours (and then examining what you find). Again, facing your dark areas is not about finding "flaws" but discovering assignments. The only shame is discovering these things and then willfully denying or ignoring them. Disregarding them allows them to grow stronger. This is your life shaking you to wake you up!

Whatever you allow, ignore, indulge in, or deny, remains in your life. Your creativity is born from who you genuinely are, and this precious gift will be filtered through and influenced by whatever is in your thoughts. The ultimate allies—or demons—in your life are your thoughts. Without careful consideration and vigilant attention to your thoughtlife, your dark side can creep up without your awareness. Once your dark side has hold of your thoughts, it can taint your ability to judge between what you love and what is destroying you. The great news is that you are in charge of your thoughtlife. No matter what anyone says or does, *you* can make decisions and take actions that will cultivate a beautiful thoughtlife. Again, I am not saying that all decisions and actions you take will be easy or perfect, but having a positive mindset can help you create a beautiful life.

We are creatures of our thinking patterns; we are led by the habits our thoughts create. We can use this for our good by deliberately focusing our attention on the positive habits that will empower us. In Chapter One, I talked about confidence being a by-product of commitment. Our thoughts are the by-products of what we mentally consume, and then think about. Simply continue feeding on, and speaking, the positive words that will create the life you desire.

When you feed your mind a healthy diet of inspiration and positivity, you will naturally develop creative, successful thought patterns, in time, generating highly original ideas that are all your own. It has been my experience that you can reach a place where you spontaneously generate creative ideas that are all your own. There are ideas in *Qreative Evolution,* for instance, that I have never seen or heard from anyone before—not even from my greatest mentors or my favorite books. But I know these concepts have emerged in my thoughts because I was ready to receive them. The great minds I have fellowshipped with throughout my life and my own self-education have strengthened my creativity and thought patterns. I truly believe that I would not have been able to discover these new ideas if it weren't for the phenomenal people I have learned from, by which I mean both from their written words or by personally encountering them.

So therefore, I encourage you to listen—even beyond the words that currently inspire you and encourage you—and discover new words that can also grow your thoughtlife with ideas that are all your own.

Your encouraging words are powerful gifts of love to yourself.

CHAPTER THREE GUIDED SELF-EDUCATION INQUIRY: YOUR EVOLUTIONARY KNOWLEDGE

1. In the section on "How to Create Your Own Curriculum," we talked about listing your desires and dreams you would like to manifest in your life. These are things you build your own curriculum around. Choose seven of these. What are they? Why have you chosen them?
2. What three books have made a seismic shift in your thinking or have had a deep impact on your life?
3. What would you add to the list of paradigm shifts like "Not Survive, But Thrive"?
4. What have you discovered as the dominant pattern of your thoughtlife?
5. Who and what triggers your dark side? How can you use the principles found in *Qreative Evolution* to immediately address your dark side?
6. Which "Life Words" do you believe you can cultivate as food for your thoughtlife?

Chapter Four

EVOLUTIONARY PRACTICE

As a lifelong work in progress, you need to deliberately establish ways to practice your best life. This chapter, "Evolutionary Practice," focuses on the process of day-to-day living. The following story illustrates how I very intentionally decided to face a fear that was limiting my growth.

Teaching was not an early aspiration of mine. For years, people had asked me if I'd ever considered teaching. "No," was always my answer. I was painfully shy and the thought of addressing a room of strangers terrified me.

But in 1994, I decided that was going to change.

I had been thinking about my eighth-grade art teacher, Mrs. Landau, and how her teaching had revolutionized my life. It occurred to me that good teachers do change lives. Realizing there must be a reason that people approached me about teaching—and there must also be a reason that I was thinking of my influential teacher, Mrs. Landau—it dawned on me that I was being given a message: Teaching was part of my life's path.

As an alum of the School of Visual Arts, I contacted them with a proposal: Would they be interested in a one-semester class on the principles of character design? I wanted to have enough time to carefully develop a curriculum, so I proposed starting the class the following year.

I was shocked when I quickly got the green light from Richard Wilde, one of SVA's chairpersons of the media arts department. He and the academic team unanimously accepted my class proposal. The school never had a course in character design before, not even in their animation department, and they were very excited to get started. There was one catch, though: They wanted me to begin that upcoming semester. At the time, it was early summer. They sent me a contract with a September start date. This gave me less than three months to prepare.

What had I gotten myself into? To say I was frightened would be an understatement. So, I decided to "feel the fear and do it anyway." The world is filled with quotes about overcoming fear, but when something really scares you, it can take more than an inspirational saying to move you out of your comfort zone. In my case, I had signed a contract to deliver a course without the year's worth of preparation I felt I needed. While I didn't feel ready to dive in so soon, I didn't want to blow this opportunity or give SVA the impression that I wasn't serious. So I said yes and got to work.

On the first day of class, I walked up the stairs to my assigned classroom, my heart beating like never before. This was not excitement. It was panic—the most crippling fear I had ever experienced.

I got to the top of the stair landing and walked to the door. I felt more and more anxiety, thinking to myself, again, *What did I get myself into?* I opened the door and saw dozens of eyes looking at me, most of them not at all impressed at seeing their new teacher. I wanted to say, "Excuse me, I'll be right back," then walk out of the building, never to return.

It didn't matter that my heart was thumping or that my students might be able to sense my fear. I was legally bound to teach this class. "Hi, everybody," I forced myself to say. "My name is Louis Henry Mitchell. Welcome to my character design class."

The fact that I didn't walk out of the building was one of my greatest triumphs. Welcoming the students was a baby step that eased the fear and kept me moving forward. The lesson went better than I thought, even though my doubts continued over the next three hours. At the end of the class, my new students were thanking me.

I went back each Friday morning for an entire semester, giving it my all and observing what I could do to teach better each week. I would practice each lecture beforehand and look for books and articles on teaching that would help me grow. I even reached out to Mrs. Landau for tips and encouragement.

By the final weeks of the fall semester, I had grown comfortable in front of the room. I had also refined my curriculum. The spring semester would start soon and I was ready to start my character design class afresh with a new batch of students and the lesson plans I'd worked so hard on. But shortly before the fall semester was over, my students began asking me to teach them more about character design. I explained that I only had one class planned—a fundamentals class—with all the basics I myself had learned about character design. They didn't care;

they were adamant about my teaching an advanced character design class the following semester.

I was summoned to the media arts department and was told that the students had signed a petition for an advanced character design class. SVA would amend my contract to teach the advanced level class, as well as the foundational course. But I was at a loss. What would I teach in an advanced class? I gave everything I had in the fundamentals class.

Or so I thought.

My desire to meet my students' request for more gave me an idea: The foundational course was about teaching the principles of character design. The advanced course could focus on the *applications* of those principles! I was extremely excited and began mapping out the advanced course over Christmas and New Year's break. Back to the resources I went, seeking more and more "food" to help me grow as I prepared to meet my students' advanced needs.

As I read, I benefited from the generosity of teachers throughout the generations who provided a banquet of educational wisdom to feast upon. So many teachers who loved what they were privileged to do prepared me for the advanced class. Although I had cultivated confidence through my commitment to teaching, this was a journey that would continue to prepare me for future teaching and lecturing opportunities that I was not yet aware of.

Facing my fear of teaching turned out to be a powerful opportunity for growth. Committing to something that frightens us expands our view of what is possible for ourselves. We become willing to say yes to opportunities we formerly couldn't see and come to regard ourselves in a new, more powerful way. Has there ever been something you wanted to do but felt unprepared for? What was it? Have you tried it? If yes, how was the experience? If not, what do you *think* was holding you back?

EVOLUTIONARY PRACTICE DEFINED

Practice living intentionally, on purpose, *right now.*

Everything you do to grow and evolve as a creative person requires perpetual and immersive practice. If you don't think you have time for perpetual and immersive practice, I want to assure you that you do. There is an easy way to constantly engage in this life-changing practice, using almost every task in your day: Intentionality. From what time you decide to go to bed, to what you choose to say yes or no to, every moment of the day is filled with opportunities to make purposeful choices in line with the purpose of your life.

You owe it to yourself to be deliberate at all times. This may seem extreme, but there is an important reason to live intentionally: The life you currently have was created from the choices of your past, many of which were made unconsciously or imposed upon you by others. Without thought. Your actions create your life whether they are planned or unplanned.

Creativity is the act of creation. It is powered by your choices. Here's one way to think about life: When engaged in a creative act—such as painting a picture—you must choose what you will portray, and what medium, colors, and brushes you will use. There are also less obvious choices you may make without thinking, such as how much pressure you use when holding the brush, or how quickly you end a brushstroke. Both the choices you make and the ones you don't think about will determine the outcome of the painting. That's why two artists using the same materials and painting the same subject matter will create two very different paintings.

Your life is also a work of art, and each choice you make—from whether to chat with someone in the elevator to what corner of an intersection to cross—puts you in a very specific place that can open you up to very specific information, resources, thoughts, memories, ideas, helpful people, inspiration, and other things that affect what you do next. You create your life using these intentional moments. Again, they are your raw material. Even something as simple as brushing your teeth could bring up an image that may influence your career choice or a project you are working on. Creation is powered by intentionality.

MORE ABOUT THE POWER OF PRACTICE

Practice is a conscious act meant to create improvement. It is a key element of creativity. It is also difficult. The mind and body *want to be* on autopilot, unconsciously doing the same thing over and over. There is a neural groove, or a thoughtlife pattern (for the brain) and a muscle memory (for the body) that are created when we make the same choices over and over. Soon, we don't even think about what we are doing—our mind or body takes over for us. This state of being on "autopilot" makes it difficult for creativity to happen. The true difference between practice and "just going through the motions" is being present, in the moment, during practice. Practice is deliberate intention. Without intention, you can miss improvements and errors.

The word practice also refers to our perpetual journey of learning and improving. A practice is an ongoing commitment. It denotes forward movement.

The phrase "living in the moment" has become almost cliché

in certain self-help circles, but it really is the best way to practice. Stay in the moment, with your choices. This will help you develop a practice mindset. When you become more accustomed to living in the moment, you will become sensitive toward the opportunities and help that are available to you. In *Qreative Evolution* I call this *serendipitous wisdom*.

HOW TO BE INTENTIONAL

If you have never lived from a place of intention, the idea of "living intentionally" may be confusing. Living this way, however, is surprisingly simple. It isn't always easy to enact, but it is simple to understand. All you must do is discover exactly what you want through honestly searching your heart, and then making choices based on what is revealed to you. I recommend being purposeful about every action in your life, from how you greet someone to what pair of socks you choose to wear. Here are a few suggestions to get you started:

- If you go to the same coffee shop each workday to grab the same breakfast, stop and think about what that breakfast is doing for your health and energy levels. Could you make a conscious choice to order something with less sugar, perhaps? Or even find a breakfast spot that specializes in healthy meals?
- When you purchase postage stamps, do you use the standard-issue flag stamp? Next

time you get stamps, select the ones with
your favorite flower or that portray a person
whom you admire.

- You walk your child to school the same way
  every day. You're not sure why—you've
  just always walked that route. Tomorrow,
  consider walking along a nearby park
  or past the community garden, or choose
  another way that makes you happy. You
  may even find some morning glories!

- Your coworker often asks if you would help
  her finish her work. You always say yes.
  You're not sure why, other than you want
  to be a team player. Next time you are
  asked, stop and think about how you should
  answer based on your workload and your
  aspirations. You may still answer yes, but
  at least that yes will have come from an
  intentional place. Or, you may say, "I'm not
  able to this week," or "No, I'm not available
  right now." Or something else.

SERENDIPITOUS WISDOM

Serendipity is "an aptitude for making desirable discoveries by
accident," which is a popular saying in the self-help world. But
the word means so much more in *Qreative Evolution*. The discoveries that you stumble upon as you navigate your unbeaten
path will reveal more and more to you, and the spirit of serendipity will grace your endeavors. You need the inefficiency

and the impracticality of challenging experiences for serendipity to appear. When things are too easy and organized, you can become trapped in a false sense of security. You start leaning on old habits instead of exploring new options. The benefit of overcoming a challenge is that you are forced to cultivate new skills. Chaos is actually an environment that you can really grow in, out of necessity.

For instance, we use computers to accomplish many things in our lives. But they can be so ridiculously efficient that you miss the serendipitous opportunities that occur around you. Steven Spielberg, a successful director who can use the highest-performing digital editing equipment available, once said he deliberately chooses not to. On the Bravo network television show, *Inside the Actors' Studio,* Spielberg revealed that he preferred editing on the old Moviola machines that used celluloid film to make match prints for editing movies. He said the time that it took to change the reels and prep for the next scene gave him time to think about what he was doing (it helped him "stay in the moment"). Modern digital editing equipment moves so fast that there wasn't time for him to think about anything before the next scene was loaded and ready for editing. His approach is not only courageous but organically evolutionary. By forcing himself to slow down, even though the nature of his business is so fast-paced, he allowed his human processes to be respected and utilized. The results of his commitment speaks for itself.

When you are exercising serendipitous wisdom, you are unable to miss anything that is truly essential to what you are doing as you create your life. You will notice things—even unusual things—that you may not initially realize are related to your life dreams. But the surprises that serendipity brings will always move you closer to your desires.

THE DIGITAL WILDERNESS

In this day and age, we face *the most* challenging mode of distraction that humanity has ever contended with: technology, specifically smartphones, computers, tablets, the internet, social media, videos, online gaming, chatrooms, apps, selfies, instant messaging, AI . . . and more.

In many cases, it looks like human development is losing out to the numbing pull of technology. That's because technology is extremely addictive. It activates the rewards center of your brain, giving a feeling of pleasure similar to alcohol or other numbing substances. While feeling good is not a bad thing at all, the desensitizing effects of technology come at a great price to our humanity. According to the informational web guide Addiction Center (www.addictioncenter.com), regular online use affects infants, children, teens, adults, and seniors in the same ways by affecting the ability to pay attention or comprehend longer or more complicated creative works, deadening creativity, minimizing sociability, and interfering with mood and sleep regulation. All of these affect a person's ability to live intentionally. It is hard to make purposeful choices for yourself when you don't have full control of your mind and body.

Let me pause first to say that I acknowledge technology's importance, power, and value. I would never suggest completely doing away with it. As human beings, we are continuously developing new and more convenient ways to engage with each other (and with ourselves). Technology can be a phenomenal tool that enhances our lives and helps us to improve ourselves.

We can connect with virtually anyone, virtually anywhere, and this ability is shrinking the world at breakneck speed. I have made new friends from all over the world, including people who have found me on some social media platform or watched one of my presentations online. I am grateful that something I said several years ago sounds brand new to someone today.

However, the speed, lack of fact-checkers, and the anonymous nature of the online world can be dangerous. Untruths, harmful messages, hateful speech, sexually predatory behavior, the dissemination of private information, misinformation, lies, and incitements to violence create an environment that can be a powerful weapon and an unforgiving trap. It is, as all things tend to be, the result of how we humans choose to use it—or allow ourselves to be used by it.

So, this part of *Qreative Evolution* is meant to help you take a deep look at technology and what it might be doing to your creativity, and to you. How often do you use technology? Is it always necessary? Would you benefit more from physically visiting your coworker rather than sending them an electronic message? Could you make a deeper connection by phoning a friend rather than commenting on their social media post? When you are curious about a topic, could you learn more by visiting a library or museum rather than relying on a quick internet search?

Many of us are losing our lives to our digital devices. I'm using the term technology broadly because even as I write this, I know there are multiple inventions being developed to make our lives more "convenient" by diminishing the physical and mental human functions we need to exercise in order to continue growing. Yet, as a work in progress, when you perform tasks—even tedious or exhausting ones—you grow. We halt our growth when we replace human tasks with technology that will do our work for us. For instance, the act of navigating a new neighborhood or city without Siri or GPS once helped us learn spatial intelligence, it strengthened our memory, and it forced us to connect with other humans in order to get where we needed to go. We no longer have to learn any of these tasks because our smartphones practically take the place of our brains.

Throughout this book, I have highlighted the ways that can enhance creativity and expand our lives. But I have also mentioned the dark side of humanity, and I believe the abuse of technology has the ability to magnify this darkness even more or even *become* that darkness. Technology reveals how willing humans are to subordinate ourselves to convenience and ease. As a result, we risk becoming addicted to, and inordinately dependent on, technology.

WHAT ABOUT OUR CHILDREN?

While *Qreative Evolution* is not a parenting book, I have to say my heart aches when I read an article like the one by Graeme Paton from *The Telegraph*, which reported this: "Rising numbers of infants lack the motor skills needed to play with building blocks because of an 'addiction' to tablet computers and smartphones, according to teachers. Many children aged three and four can 'swipe a screen' but have little to no dexterity in their fingers after spending hours glued to iPads, it was claimed."

In 2002, Katy Kelly wrote an article entitled

"False Promises," that said, "Too much 'screen time' at a young age, they say, may undermine the development of critical skills that kids need to become successful, diminishing creativity and imagination, motivation, attention spans, and the desire to persevere."

I encourage you to interact with your children one-on-one, free of technology as much as possible. Let me share a story about how I did this with my son.

One Saturday afternoon, Michaelanthony asked me, "Hey Dad, how many teeth does a T. rex have?"

I told him we should do some research on the subject and find out. When he heard the word "research," he immediately walked over to his computer, which I kept in my studio rather than his bedroom.

"No, Mike," I said, "let's go to the Museum of Natural History and find out."

"But Dad, we can find out easily with a computer search."

"Yes, we can," I replied. "But that will give us information from someone else's research. It's always worth the effort to learn from your own observations."

At the museum, Michaelanthony found the head of a T. rex low enough to the floor so that he could count all its teeth himself. The joy in his eyes was something I will carry with me for life. After that, he was thrilled to—serendipitously—discover

that polar bears have black skin like a scuba suit
and their fur is not white but made up of thin hollow
tubes that reflect light and work as heat collectors
to help them stay warm. I am proud to say that to
this day, my son continues to look further than his
computer when he is learning something new.

PRACTICING LIFE

Our DNA is ancient. While humankind benefits from technological advances, what we can do as human beings is what keeps us functioning properly. Using your natural memory is vital to the continued development of your brain. Something as simple as memorizing phone numbers and punching in the individual digits may seem frivolous today, but every way you exercise your brain will stimulate it to function as it is meant to function. When you give it less to do, you move away from processes that make you human.

"... yeah, yeah, but your scientists were so preoccupied with whether or not they could that they didn't stop to think whether or not they should."
—IAN MALCOLM, FICTIONAL CHARACTER
FROM *JURASSIC PARK*

Be intentional. Practice life. Live on purpose. Use your brain and your body and the deeper parts of who you are as they were intended to be used. Technology is a wonderful tool as long as it is treated as a tool and not as an ultimate answer. It should not be allowed to be a replacement for the functions your brain is meant to do. "Use it or lose it" still, and always will, apply.

CREATING HARMONY BETWEEN HUMANITY AND TECHNOLOGY

In Chapter Three, we explored the difference between balance and harmony. The tug-of-war of humanity versus technology lends itself well to this concept. First, it's important to admit that technology is never going away. And yet, it's essential that we are honest with ourselves about the ways that technology distracts us from our creativity, from our goals, from each other, and from our humanness. It suppresses our ability to have human experiences that will help us grow, make memories, and change the way we see ourselves for the better.

Creating, connecting, exploring, learning—in real time, in person—is how we as a species are designed to grow. Your creativity—the very thing that you use to create your life—relies on your ability to be in the present moment. Just you, and the experience that you are engaging in, whether it's a walk through the park, practicing the piano, or swinging in a hammock with a book. Synapses are formed, muscle memories are made, connections are built, and opportunities are created when you engage in life with no electronic crutch. Again, I ask you to profoundly think about your technology use.

Demonizing technology is not my intent here. I am simply expressing my concern for how overdependent we are on it and how it can disrupt necessary human functions. It certainly can be used in productive and creative ways that support and assist us with our day-to-day necessities. A great example of this is how technology helped me to expedite a social media project for

Women's History Month. I was asked to create an illustration of the Muppet Zoe based on the famous "Rosie the Riveter" poster symbolizing women in the workforce and women's independence back in the 1940s. However, the request was for a full-color illustration rather than the kind of drawing I traditionally did in black and white on paper. There wasn't enough time for me to do a color painting, so I opted to do it as a digital illustration. Instead of acrylic paint, I set out to use Adobe Photoshop to create it. I used the same kind of strokes that I would have used with a paintbrush, but I used a stylus instead on a touch-sensitive monitor. There was no time taken to mix the paints because I just chose the official colors of Zoe from the digital library of colors normally used to create the illustrated version of her. So, using pixels instead of paint cut the time by three-quarters. Because I studied traditional painting, the digital illustration looked as if it had been done with paint. I used technology to support my traditional way of creating, combining them both, but keeping the technology as the support, not the main technique.

Most people have to take physical precautions to keep themselves away from technology so they can learn, explore, and engage in humanity. Silencing your phone or moving your laptop to another room shows you are willing to do what it takes to remove distractions so you can engage in the activities that will in turn create the life you came here to live.

In addition to designating intentional *daily* "tech-free" time, it can help to add in more and more human experiences. Tap into the ancient wisdom of your DNA. Set your human hand on the task before you, solve problems with your mind, feel the wind in your hair and the rain on your face, smell the flowers.

Do human things. This is where you will resonate with the living thread of your creative spirit. No matter how much anyone tries, no one will ever be able to truly resonate with a machine.

With this in mind, we can benefit from the wisdom of those who, undistracted by excessive technology, furthered human development with the thoughts they left behind. These great minds left us so much to ponder, so we would not forget who we are and what we could intentionally become. They were deeper thinkers, who excavated the human psyche to find solutions for living. Here are some examples of what they had to say:

Hypatia of Alexandria (AD 370–415): "Understanding the things that surround us is the best preparation to understand the things that lie beyond."

M. de Voltaire (1694–1778): "Appreciation is a wonderful thing: It makes what is excellent in others belong to us as well."

Ralph Waldo Emerson (1803–1882): "Our greatest glory is not in never failing, but in rising up every time we fail."

Frederick Douglass (1818–1895): "It is easier to build strong children than to repair broken men."

Edith Stein (1891–1942): "The entire educational process must be carried out with love, which is perceptible in every disciplinary measure and which does not instill any fear. And the most effective educational method is not the word of instruction but the living example without which all words remain useless."

This list could go on for hundreds of pages thanks to the multitude of individuals who contributed to humankind's legacy. Invest in yourself and reach back in time to the gifts that were prepared for us. When I encourage people to look to the thinkers of yesteryear, I am sometimes met with resistance. Some people don't want to learn from people who perhaps lived in or as part of a shameful era. To that, I say, yes, things occurred in the past that brought great shame to humankind and showed the baseness of human behavior. But looking throughout human history—which means considering the cultural context, belief systems, and social mores—can help us see the benevolence that I still believe is the core of humanity. At our core, I believe we are all artists creating our lives. And with that in mind, I would like to turn next to the *Qreative Evolution* way of seeing the elements of art as they may occur in our daily lives.

THE FOUR CREATIVE ARTS

Because I believe we are meant to live our lives as our personal work of art, I look at everyone's life through an artistic lens. So wherever "artists" are mentioned in *Qreative Evolution*, it applies to everyone. Each of us is an artist.

When I looked deeply at how the arts all come together, I believe that there are ultimately four creative art forms. The number four is a very significant number in history, creativity, and nature. Biblically, it was on the fourth day that the four materials for the earth were created: the sun, the moon, the stars, and the "heavenly bodies," or the universe. There are four great elements: earth, air, fire, and water. The four directions are north, south, east, and west. The four seasons of the year are winter, spring, summer, and fall. There are four phases to the moon: new moon, first quarter, full moon, and third quarter. Each day has four distinct divisions: morning, noon, evening, and night.

I wanted to highlight the number four here as I share what I discovered about the creative arts. This is the *Qreative Evolution* focus on how these four art forms complement each other. Looking at them this way revealed more than I had ever anticipated.

I saw how unlimited they are individually and how they work together to create a stream of creative expression.

Literary Arts: Written expression, general and creative writing, journalism, speeches, poetry, letters, etc.

Visual Arts: Graphic expression, drawing, sculpture, painting, graphic design, architectural design, etc.

Performing Arts: Physical artistic expression, singing, dancing, film, puppetry, cooking, sports, and many other activities far too numerous to list here. The point being that this is about personal active expressions which stem from physical creative expression.

Communication Arts: Public speaking, teaching, psychology, therapy, marketing, public relations, etc. This art form is the thread that weaves all the others together. This is the one that reveals everyone is an artist because we are all in the act of communicating. Many of us don't communicate well, however, because we aren't invested in becoming the best communicators we can be.

Each of the Four Creative Arts flow together in simplicity and symbiotic grace. Think of a baker who would thoughtfully write out a cake recipe (literary), imagine, perhaps in a sketch, how to present the cake (visual), mix and bake the cake with great care (performance), and serve it to those who will enjoy it (communication). All four can apply to any area of life. When intentionally applying all four arts, there is a completeness that occurs through the careful and deliberate attention applied.

For the majority of my creative life, I drew, painted, sculpted, and designed puppets, as well as played the piano. Writing, however, was not something I thought much about, as I didn't feel I could excel in it. When Chief Curator at the Norman Rockwell

Museum Stephanie Plunkett asked me to write a blog for the museum's website, I decided to learn what I could about writing well. I got more practice when I was asked to write some of the plaques accompanying the art on the museum walls, and then to pen the foreword to the book about Norman Rockwell's drawings. I never saw any of this coming.

What I believe supported me as a writer was being allowed to write about something I loved: Art. In my writing for the Norman Rockwell Museum, I used the written word to communicate my love of his art.

Life is a journey, and as we courageously grow and evolve, we discover opportunities that help shape and refine us. I was nervous about writing for my favorite artist's museum, but I realized the growth opportunity that it was and accepted the invitation. I had no idea I would excel to the degree I did because of the kindness, support, and generosity of Mrs. Plunkett. The Four Creative Arts have become the infrastructure and the texture of my life as an artist. Through them I learned that my "job" was not to decide how to be creative, but to *discover* how creativity is revealed through me.

There are most likely at least two forms of creative expression within you. Explore and learn which forms you gravitate toward. Your relationship with each of these art forms influences your interactions with the others. Sometimes while I am at the piano I am unintentionally working out a drawing in my head while I play. The same goes for when I am at my drawing table and music is flowing in my head. Sometimes it is when I am clipping the hedges in my front yard. I love to cut the hedges as sculpture and it feels great when my neighbors observe me doing it with so much love as I perform with the clippers. They ask me how I get the shapes so precise and I get to talk with them, communicating my love for clipping my hedges. What seems to be a mundane chore becomes a visual show for my neighbor's pleasure, as well as an opportunity to create. To be honest, when I approach cutting the hedges this way, I am able to enjoy the same excitement as when I am drawing or playing the piano. It is about being intentional toward making every possible part of my life another work of my art.

As you look at your own creative expression through the scaffolding of the Four Creative Arts you will see the natural overlaps and intimate connections throughout your daily life. It's what you learn and know about yourself that carries through what you set your hand to.

REPLACEMENT THERAPY

I believe the most effective way to eliminate bad habits is to replace them with good habits. I call this "replacement therapy." Habits are behaviors—they can be helpful, harmful, or neutral—that you have engaged in so frequently that your brain creates what is called a neural pathway. This is like the old familiar route you take to work each day, the one that you travel without even thinking. A habit lightens your brain's workload by removing the need to participate in decision-making. Instead, the brain just copies the behavior encoded in the neural pathway, saving excess energy to use elsewhere. This brings us back to how we cultivate our thoughtlife.

Identify the unhelpful habits you have. Examining why you have developed these behaviors, where each of them came from, and how they currently harm you, is a form of self-care. Do not judge yourself: This is another place to use your creativity toward the evolution of your life.

Once you discover a behavior that is not serving you or your purpose in life, you have found not a "flaw" but a new assignment. Not all habits are negative. Consider positive habits that you could develop to enhance your life, habits that would help you function on a higher level.

I'll give you an example of replacement therapy from my own life. At one time, I was hooked on coffee and wanted to stop my dependence on caffeine. So, I learned to replace my daily coffee with bone broth and it has made a miraculous difference. Coffee is an occasional treat. Yes, bone broth is more expensive than coffee and takes more effort to make, or to find. But I shifted my perspective and replaced my "pick-me-up" addiction with a "build-me-up" investment.

"Creativity lives in health. It is faked in sickness."
—LOUIS HENRY MITCHELL

CREATIVE ACCESS COMES THROUGH CLEAN LIVING

Drugs and alcohol don't make people more creative. They simply distort, taint, and basically ruin the intellectual, creative, and spiritual access you're meant to have with your true self. Accidental "genius" is what we see when someone who is drunk or high accomplishes something on a seemingly high creative level. They gave up who they truly are, leaving their creative gift to chance under the influence.

A healthy spirit, mind, and body creates the creativity trinity. A mind and body influenced and warped by chemical alterations yields counterfeit creativity. Using legal or illegal substances to ignite creativity is generally an attempt to avoid, or subdue, anxiety. I don't blame anyone for attempting to lessen or eliminate anxiety, but there are ways to do this without self-destruction. If you experience anxiety (or anything that affects your ability to self-regulate, such as depression, anger issues, attention deficits, learning disorders, processing disorders, etc.), please give yourself the gift of help. Find the best professional help you can, as you learn how to care for your well-being. For virtually every problem there is help available now.

"Attitude is a choice. Happiness is a choice. Optimism is a choice. Kindness is a choice. Giving is a choice. Respect is a choice. Whatever choice you make makes you. Choose wisely."

—ROY T. BENNETT

CHAPTER FOUR GUIDED SELF-EDUCATION INQUIRY: YOUR EVOLUTIONARY PRACTICE

1. What recurring themes or situations do you notice that have a significant serendipitous meaning in your life?

2. In what specific ways do you realize you've been distracted by technology?

3. What beneficial human functions could you be doing that you've allowed technology to take over?

4. How would you rearrange "The Four Creative Arts" to represent yourself?

5. What ancient wisdom and practices that existed before the advent of technology do you currently use to ground yourself?

6. Find wisdom from those who lived before technology became a distraction. Explore their writings for quotes that inspire you.

Chapter Five
EVOLUTIONARY FELLOWSHIP

In this chapter, we will talk about the importance of discovering your tribe. There has been a lot written about being part of a "tribe." However, through *Qreative Evolution*, we will explore it to make it even more uniquely specific to your journey. You'll learn how to identify the people who are truly with you and those who are not. It isn't always obvious who is or is not in your corner. We have historically been programmed to accept or excuse the behavior of people in our lives, even when that behavior is detrimental to our happiness, our purpose, or even our lives. Friends who should be supportive may undermine your success, while some individuals you have just met may become your greatest champions. In this next story, I share how supportive people influenced my early development, which not only impacted my career success but continues to positively influence me today.

MY ROAD TO THE NORMAN ROCKWELL MUSEUM
Even though I never met Norman Rockwell, I feel that he has been mentoring me from my early experiences in the art field

to later in my work for *Sesame Street*. Even when I am direct-ing Muppet photo shoots, the lessons of composition and visual storytelling I learned from Rockwell influence every scene. His ability to tell stories with images is a kind of superpower that has deeply influenced me. In this way, you may say that Rock-well has been mentoring me since I was sixteen years old.

I had earned my way into the High School of Art and Design, an art-focused high school in Manhattan. The school was not easy to get into, and being accepted was a tremendous boost to my confidence.

After an exciting—and intimidating—first day of art high school, I went to the neighborhood around the school in search of food and spotted a McDonald's across the street. As I ap-proached it, I noticed a small bookstore next to it. Wondering if they sold art books, I went inside. The bookstore owner pointed up toward a higher level of the shop, where I saw books on Pi-casso, Hockney, Pollock, and so many more.

As I was browsing through the stacks, something caught my eye. Was it a painting? A drawing? Something else? It looked so realistic. I picked it up and saw that it was a painting by some-one named Norman Rockwell. It was the first time I had ever seen his work. Eventually I learned that the image on the cover called *Freedom from Want* was one of his famous Four Freedoms paintings. The book was entitled *Norman Rockwell Illustrator*. On each page were images of the most realistic-looking draw-ings and paintings I had ever seen.

That little bookstore became my real art school. I went there every weekday after school, just to look through the Norman Rockwell book. I couldn't afford it because it was a whole $4.95, plus tax, and I didn't dare use my lunch money to buy it. But with each passing day, the desire to own the book grew stronger, until I decided that it would be worth it to skip a few lunches so I could save up and buy that treasure.

One day when I went to look through the book, just like I did every day, the book was gone. I panicked. "Excuse me, sir," I said to the store owner. "Where is that book I always look at?"

"Oh," said the owner. "Someone bought it."

I was horrified. I almost had enough money to buy it. When the bookstore owner saw the look on my face, he immediately said, "But I have another one in the back." He almost ran to get it for me.

I asked if he'd hold it for me until I could purchase it a few days later. That man was like an angel to me. He never chased me away or impatiently asked me if I was going to buy it. He just let me enjoy it every single day.

I'm sure my mother wondered why my appetite was more robust than usual on the days I skipped lunch. I could have asked her for the money and I'm sure she would have found a way to give it to me. But she was a single mother who worked full-time as a nurse and managed a small apartment building, never charging the kind of rent she could have in order to help some people out. Her generosity meant she often had to add money to our mortgage, because she didn't earn a profit.

After I was able to purchase that book, I started seeing other books and calendars featuring Norman Rockwell's artwork. When my brother-in-law brought me to a bookstore in the Kings Plaza Shopping Mall in Brooklyn, I immediately found a huge volume entitled *Norman Rockwell: Artist and Illustrator*. It was the biggest book I had ever seen, and it was loaded with more pictures than the book I had just purchased.

Plus, some of the pages showed full-color, actual-size details from some of his most famous paintings. However, that book cost *eighty-one dollars.*

I knew not to even think about asking my brother-in-law. So, I went to my mother and pleaded, "I really need it, Mom."

"Eighty-one dollars for one book?" she asked incredulously. Her reply was not unreasonable for 1977. I didn't want to push, but I had to have that masterpiece.

About three days later, my mother came home from work and told me that I could get the book. I hugged her like I never had before. My tears were staining her uniform, but she didn't care. She knew that book would help me, but neither of us realized how much.

That book was followed by several other Rockwell books. I even found one at the book sale at the local public library entitled *My Adventures as an Illustrator*. It was a biographical account written with the help of Thomas Rockwell, the second of Norman Rockwell's three sons. It wasn't in great shape, so the library was selling it for a single dollar. After I bought it, I noticed Norman Rockwell's autograph in the book. It was a collector's item.

I share all of this to emphasize what a Norman Rockwell fan I was (and still am). But I went from being a fan to much more. Fast forward to the day I was drawing some *Sesame Street* Muppets when I received a phone call from someone in our publishing department. She needed a detailed set of instructions on how to pose Cookie Monster for a temporary exhibit. I answered that I would be happy to travel to the exhibit and pose Cookie Monster myself, but I was told this was at "a museum far out of town."

When I asked which museum, the woman said, "The Norman Rockwell Museum, in Stockbridge, Massachusetts." She knew I loved Rockwell but said she didn't want to "tease" me by divulging all the details. No matter—if *Sesame Street* was sending my favorite of all the Muppet characters (I love Cookie Monster) to my favorite artist's museum, it was a sign. I *had* to go.

I was told there was no budget to send me. "I'll pay my own way," I answered. (To my delight, they did end up finding money to fund my trip.).

I arrived at the exhibit to find Cookie Monster—an actual Muppet that had appeared on *Sesame Street* before it was retired from extensive wear—on display in the rear of the museum, near the other *Sesame Street* memorabilia. The exhibit was named "From Woodstock to the Moon," and it celebrated how *Sesame Street*, The Norman Rockwell Museum, Woodstock, and the Apollo 11 moon landing all "launched" in 1969.

Even though he was holding a cookie, Cookie Monster looked sad. He drooped forward. Thankfully, the exhibit had just opened so I was able to get to him before the public saw him in such a state. I asked the museum staff to quickly remove the plexiglass cover. I took ahold of him, straightened his posture, and then posed him with a big smile. (In case you're wondering how I made Cookie Monster smile, there was some flexibility in the Muppet's face that allowed me to turn up the corners of his mouth.) That was the Cookie Monster we all knew and loved!

Many visitors became emotional when they saw one of *Sesame Street*'s most beloved characters. While I was enjoying the responses of the crowd, the museum's deputy director and chief curator, Stephanie Plunkett, asked if this is what I did for

Sesame Workshop. I told her it was among the many things I was privileged to do.

"Would you consider doing a lecture at our museum about your work for *Sesame Street*?" she asked me.

I was stunned. I was being asked to talk at my favorite artist's museum! Of course, I said yes. I returned to the museum and gave my lecture. Afterward, I stood with Stephanie inside Rockwell's studio, which had been moved onto the museum grounds in 1986. When Stephanie asked what the museum could do for me in gratitude, I asked her as humbly as possible, "May I sit in Mr. Rockwell's chair?"

"Oh, we often get that request," said Stephanie. "We never let anyone sit in his chair. But, for you, Louis, we can make an exception. We'll set it up for you tomorrow."

I wasn't sure I heard that right, but Stephanie assured me that she'd be delighted to accommodate me. I was welcomed the very next morning. His studio looked just as it did when he worked there. I looked quickly around, half expecting him to appear. It felt like Mr. Rockwell had quickly left his desk to get a bottle of Coca-Cola, his favorite drink, and would be back any minute. I will never forget when Stephanie said those wonderful words, "Have a seat, Louis."

I slowly walked toward the chair, sat down for about five seconds, and said a heartfelt, "Thank you."

As I was getting up, she said, "No, Louis. Stay there. Where's your phone? Let me take some pictures of you." I was shaking as she snapped several photos. It all meant so much to me. I thanked her again as I got up, and she continued taking photos of me as I studied Rockwell's personal items and art supplies. It was among the greatest days of my life.

If the story ended here it would be perfect. But then I had an idea. I learned that Rockwell kept many of his fan letters. I asked Stephanie if the museum happened to have the letter I sent to Rockwell when I was eighteen years old. She promised to check.

On my next visit to the museum—about three months later—Stephanie walked me to the library. On one of the counters were two sheets of paper. One of them was the very letter I had written to Norman Rockwell in April 1978, shortly before he died. The other was a pristine copy, which the museum had framed for me. I was stunned with gratitude.

As Stephanie and I spoke, I noticed a gentleman standing immediately to my left. He enthusiastically introduced himself as Peter Williams and asked if he could buy me a cup of coffee. We went to the museum café where he told me he was the chair of the committee of trustees. "Would you consider becoming a member of our board of trustees?" he asked.

I happily accepted, in awe of the avalanche of gifts I had received, all connecting me to my favorite artist. But there was more to come. I suggested to Stephanie there should be a book focused on Norman Rockwell's drawings, as he always had said that drawing was his favorite part of his illustration process. A year later, Stephanie excitedly told me that Abbeville Press had agreed to publish this book, *Norman Rockwell Drawings, 1911–1976*. "Louis, we would love for you to write the book's introduction," she said.

My own special tribute to Norman Rockwell, in a book about my favorite part of his work? Stephanie gave me four months to write it. I finished it that weekend. Some time had passed when Stephanie sent me a mockup of the book's cover.

In its lower left corner were these words: "Foreword by Louis Henry Mitchell." I was thrilled.

It isn't just Rockwell's art that moves me. It is Rockwell the man. He was a sensitive, gifted, and conscientious human being who was devoted to showing the dignity of *all* people. Some of my favorite Rockwell paintings include *The Problem We All Live With*, which focuses on Ruby Bridges, the first African American child to desegregate William Frantz Elementary School in New Orleans. Rockwell also painted *The Golden Rule*, which shows people of various races and cultures together. He was a lifetime member of the NAACP, and he posthumously helped represent Vice President Kamala Harris, the first woman, the first Black American, and the first South Asian American to be elected to this position, when artist Bria Goeller designed an image featuring Harris casting a shadow on a wall. The shadow was not Harris, but Rockwell's Ruby Bridges.

Throughout this adventure, I discovered that Stephanie Plunkett was revealed as being a member of my personal tribe. If he were alive, I would like to think that Norman Rockwell would have been, too.

WHAT IS A TRIBE, AND WHY DO YOU NEED ONE?

Your tribe is a group of supportive people you can count on. It is made up of mentors, mentees, supportive family members, neighbors, and many other people you may encounter. These are unique people who reveal themselves as members of your tribe. They create fellowship, lift you up, look out for you, cheer you on, and let you do the same for them. Your tribe is your inner circle, your *discovered* family, and we will get more into what that word "family" means through the *Qreative Evolution* lens shortly. When you can rely on people and they can rely on you, your tribe has been revealed. Sometimes you might doubt yourself, but that's the time when your trusted inner circle can help you move forward by ensuring that you don't give up on your purpose.

We will explore how to discover who your actual tribe is a bit later in this chapter, but for now, let's understand why you need a tribe. Right now, think about who is in your corner. Who do you feel you can *really* count on? Who shares passions that are similar to yours? Who do you feel compelled to support as a member of their tribe?

LOCATE YOUR MENTORS

Mentors are individuals within your tribe who bring a special level of support to you. Again, we are exploring the terms used in this book to help you look for the deeper meanings *Qreative Evolution* brings out. You will discover who can actually have more of a leadership role in your particular journey. A tribe member can be someone you partner with or someone you are guiding because they need your help. Then there are those tribe members who challenge you and help you grow with the trust they have earned in your life. These guides are here to educate you, help you think and do things, and keep you moving forward. Any individual who inspires and motivates you is your revealed mentor. You may have more than one mentor, and you may also find that certain people act as mentors in very specific areas of your life. Perhaps you have a career mentor, a financial mentor, a mentor who guides you to be a more present parent, a wellness mentor who encourages you to attend to your health.

Allowing yourself to be mentored is not about worshipping fellow human beings. It's about observing and appreciating them for their wisdom, their knowledge, and their willingness to share their insights with others.

As a reminder, mentors are not always people you know personally. I have many mentors I haven't yet met and some I will never meet, but I appreciate their intellect and how generously they share with others through their books, podcasts, documentaries, service work, and more. Furthermore, mentors don't have to be living. I have learned so much about building a strong character, mindset, artistic skills, spirituality, and more from individuals who are no longer with us. I consider Norman Rockwell, Jim Henson, and Martin Luther King Jr., for instance, to be my mentors because the wisdom they have so generously shared continues to educate and guide me.

In fact, Dr. Martin Luther King Jr.—one of my life mentors in spirit—contributed the very first element of the *Qreative Evolution* curriculum. I was watching the news reports on the sixteenth anniversary of Dr. King's death, holding my son in my arms, and as Dr. King delivered his sermon "The Three Dimensions of a Complete Life," it sent me to a time and place I could never have gone otherwise. As a matter of fact, I highly recommend finding and reading the entire sermon for yourself.

> **"You should do your job and do it so well, that the living, the dead, or the unborn couldn't do it any better."**
>
> **—MARTIN LUTHER KING JR.**

THE HUMANITY OF MENTORS

Have you ever researched someone you admire, only to feel so intimidated by their accomplishments and success that you wonder if your own dreams are even possible? If so, you are not alone. On my journey to learn more about my mentors, I read books and articles and watched anything I could find on them (remember, I grew up in the days before the internet, so research for me looked different than it may for you).

In trying to learn more about how my mentors achieved success, I found very little information about the struggles they overcame. Most of the material focused on my mentors' achievements and the wonderful highlights of their lives. I often found that their lives seemed too perfect. In my heart I knew there must have been some challenges they had to overcome, just like all human beings have challenges to overcome. I knew that hardship plays a large part in shaping a person, and I was hoping to learn something from them that could help me in my own journey.

So I started to dig deeper into their lives, searching for any information about the struggles my mentors had to overcome. I went to the library looking for answers anywhere I could find them, including biographies, old news clippings, videos, and anything that could tell me how my mentors grew into who they became.

After much research, I learned that in Martin Luther King Jr.'s life, he suffered extreme doubt about being the leader of the civil rights movement. In *Stride Toward Freedom: The Montgomery Story*, Dr. King shares how he agonized over his fear. He talks about the burden of fear and whether or not he was up to the job of leading the charge. He was scared that he would not live up to people's expectations or meet the demands of such an enormous assignment. "It seemed that all my fears had come down on me at once . . . And I got to the point that I couldn't take it any longer. I was weak." He not only questioned it, but he considered rejecting the call. This showed me that one of my mentors—even though he seemed so heroic, so "larger than life" to me—was a regular human being with regular human frailties. It's not that I wanted to know Dr. King had hardships in his life, but I *needed* to know that he faced challenges in his life like we all do. So no matter how famous or celebrated someone is for their accomplishments, you should always look deeper to learn what they had to go through to get there.

THE POWER OF HUMAN CONTACT

The further away we get from interacting with other humans—from visits and walks and in-person chats—the further away we get from being fully human.

Participating in humanity can be as simple as just saying hello to a coworker (or even a stranger) in the morning. I love how children so freely say hello to me when they see me in the park or just walking down the street. Although I don't engage with them unless I know their parents are aware of it, I will always smile whenever a child smiles at me. It also reminds me of myself in an earlier time. Six-year-old Louis remains my greatest mentor of all.

Courteous gestures are genuine manifestations of humanity. They are superpowers, mostly because only a few do them. I encounter far more rude people than I do friendly ones. To me, rudeness isn't just giving a nasty look or spouting an expletive. It can also be just ignoring another person as if they didn't exist.

Those who embrace their humanity and acknowledge how vital community is tap into deeper and more fulfilling creative experiences that involve actual human contact. For instance, the appreciation I'm given when someone receives a handwritten letter from me truly touches my heart. I have made a vow to myself that I will never send out another e-card. It's either a real handwritten card or a phone call, and I will keep trying until I get the actual person and speak *with* them.

"You can tell the quality of a person by what they do with their freedom and how they respond to the human community through it."
—LOUIS HENRY MITCHELL

SOME ARE YOUR PEOPLE AND SOME ARE NOT

As I move through life, I discover many beautiful people who are uniquely connected with me. Their mere presence in my life brings out the best in me. These valuable companions are meant to receive me and be received by me.

The gratitude I have for my own personal tribe is immeasurable. It takes a long time to cultivate a tribe and, again, they are revealed to you, not chosen. I've mentioned my mother many times throughout this book. She was the head of my tribe as I grew up until I became the head myself. Her love and her voice, which keeps her alive in my heart, are ever-present in my life. My son, Michaelanthony, is certainly a high-ranking member and, as I mentioned before, among my greatest teachers. Rabbi Simon Jacobson, who wrote my favorite book, started as a mentor exclusively from what I learned from his book. He became a member of my tribe after I wrote to him for permission to use the picture of those two pages I highlighted previously. I shared how much his book meant to me, and he requested a meeting after reading my heartfelt explanation. We bonded within an hour of the first meeting.

The former CEO of Lindblad Expeditions and, as of this writing, the chairman of the Norman Rockwell Museum board of directors, Dolf Berle, revealed himself to such a degree that we count each other as brothers. Rachel Lunden-Carter, the former intern from Sesame Workshop, who saw it in me to be able to work with children on the spectrum, is far more than just a friend. She is among my most treasured tribe members who saw something in me I could never have seen in myself. But she took the time to learn how to help me understand the love I have for children and how it was all I needed. She taught me how to be part of the lives of those children with autism, leading to the very reason and validation for my designing the Julia Muppet for *Sesame Street*. There are many very precious people who have made a lasting mark in different parts of my life. But these and some other very, very special ones, many of whom who I didn't even see coming, were revealed as true members of my tribe.

The discovery of your tribe is unique to you. No one else can choose them for you and it will most likely not be a very large group. Again they are revealed to you, one by one, over time, and the gauge is how they choose to contribute to your life. Who are the people in your tribe? Are you able to have the patience to allow them to be revealed to you rather than trying to choose them for yourself and possibly make the wrong choices? This is, of course, not about seeking "perfect" tribe members. It's about discovering those who genuinely rise to the occasion of bringing true love and support that is always present, even when they aren't with you. The feeling of knowing they are in your corner and will go to extraordinary lengths to give you support is a driving force to you. And value your contributions to their lives, showing you that you are in this life together and that you are never alone when you acknowledge your true tribe.

People will enter your life, spend time in it, and then exit. This is as it should be. But members of your tribe will remain in your life—and you in theirs—with *clear evidence* of their connection to you and with you. Simply by having them in your life, you are improved. The problem occurs when we allow people who are not good for us (or our lives), to get close to us. We may confuse their role in our lives and allow them access to us that they should not have. Having the wrong people near you can slow your progress, take you off track and harm you emotionally, and sometimes physically and spiritually.

> Be mindful of who you allow into your inner tribal circle. The devastatingly high price of being thrown off track by their negativity is never worth paying. They are among the naysayers who do not get a vote in your life.

You must be intimately aware of the people in your life. I want to say something difficult here: Not everyone who enters your life should remain in your life. We were not put on this planet to be discouraged, frightened, harmed, or oppressed by anyone. But it is not always easy to tell who these people are. This is why it is important to learn ways to acknowledge those who choose to deplete and diminish life by passive-aggressive means, neglect, violence, or a negative attitude. Sometimes a therapist can help us identify these people and work with us to set up healthy boundaries.

Cleansing and refining your life is essential to your growth.

It is also an ongoing process. To create your "best life," you must protect it and learn to identify the removable obstacles that will keep you from growing and moving forward. Often these road-blocks appear in the form of people. It could be a needy friend who constantly distracts you with texts and phone calls. It could be the neighbor who makes it difficult to move easily in and out of your home. It could be acquaintances who spew intolerance online. It could be a naysayer, a put-down artist, a narcissist, a gossip, a trash-talker, or someone who is frightened to do some-thing on their own who is always calling you "for help." Or it could be someone else who stands in the way of your progress.

There are so many wonderful people in the world who make their lives and the lives of others things of beauty. Re-gardless of the challenges that they may face, these people enjoy the journey of life as the celebration it is. If you know people like this, hold them close as they are far more valuable than gold. I believe that we attract these people when we commit to being our best genuine selves. You've probably heard the saying "like attracts like." If I want to connect with individuals who embrace life, the best way to do that is to openly live this way myself.

> Live positively, and those who spread negativity and have no regard for life will instinctively move away from you. Your enthusiasm will make them uncomfortable. If they *do not* remove themselves, you need to move away from them. Be careful who you share your life with because not everyone will support you, based on who you are and what you are here to accomplish.

Believe it or not, negative people are not flawed. As I mentioned before, those negative people are individuals who have ignored their gifts and their assignments as works in progress. Unfortunately, however, no amount of positivity from others will transform the negative people in the world to positive people. Only they themselves—if they truly desire to change—can create this transformation.

We need to be accountable for our own lives. We also need to hold other people accountable for who they've decided to be in our lives (and who they've decided you are in theirs). Once you become aware of what is obstructing your creativity and your very life, you must make the efforts necessary to deal with that obstruction. So I recommend to you that you ignore these people, avoid them, stay positive, tell them how you feel, or get professional help in how to handle them. Find a way to move around and past them.

THE LIFE POWER OF FORGIVENESS
AND RELEASING GRUDGES

Now, we go from the tribe of people who make positive contributions to your life to those who haven't learned how to. This is where one of our greatest human endowments comes into play: forgiveness. Forgiving someone is one of the most intentional, most challenging, purpose-filled actions you may ever take. When someone wrongs you—perhaps they sabotage your success, neglect you, harm you, lie to you, or behave in any targeted negative way toward you—it is understandable to feel a range of uncomfortable emotions, such as rage, despair, sadness, anguish, confusion, terror, depression, humiliation, shame, or fear, to name just a few. Unfortunately, it is normal to feel these things on a regular basis, meaning we, the wronged, have not only been hurt by someone, we also are affected by our own wounded feelings of the event. That is a lot of time spent feeling negative. It is hard to live in the moment while being held hostage by these heavy feelings.

Forgiveness lets you put down the heavy feelings so you can focus on your growth rather than any darkness you feel about what happened to you. Research studies have found that forgiveness is good for the forgiver. One of these studies, published in the March 2001 issue of *Association for Psychological Science*, was performed by researchers at Hope College in Holland, Michigan. The psychological stress or relaxation responses of seventy-one participants were measured when they were faced with hurtful memories of something a person or persons did which they had not yet forgiven, as well as when they were asked about examples of forgiveness toward their real-life offenders. When asked about their grudges, participants showed high levels of psychological stress. When asked to think about instances of forgiveness, study participants felt calm and showed no stress. This study shows how forgiveness can help you feel better in the moment. Other studies have shown the longer-term benefits of forgiveness. Those who forgive a wrongdoer experience lower levels of anxiety, depression, and hostility. They are less likely to self-medicate with substances. They show higher levels of self-esteem and even greater life satisfaction, all of which can help you focus on the good you are here to do.

If you find forgiveness difficult, start small. Forgive the person who does not thank you for holding the door or giving way on the sidewalk. Do this daily until forgiving larger transgressions becomes easier. Reaching out to a counselor is also helpful. Working with a therapist can help you heal your wounds and give you a different outlook on whatever happened.

Keep in mind, and in your heart, that it's not what others do to you that has the greatest impact on you; It's your *response* to the challenge that makes it something you can learn and grow from. Unforgiveness—living in the state of not forgiving—is not a flaw. It is another assignment being revealed to you. Addressing it will help further your own personal growth. And the very best person to start forgiveness with is yourself.

"People teach you how to treat them."
—DONNA CHANDLER

PURSUE YOUR PURPOSE AND THE RIGHT SUPPORT APPEARS

As I've said throughout this book, I see creativity as the act of creating a life. In other words, it is the life force with which you create not just art but your very life. Part of creating a life is learning from other humans. Every time you interact with another person—even in passing—you have the opportunity to learn something. This learning can then be used creatively to create something. While we are not here to force connections with those with whom we don't naturally connect, we can still learn *something* from them, even if it is what to avoid.

More pleasant lessons, however, come from those with whom we resonate. Making deep connections with supportive, positive people is not only gratifying; it helps us feel braver so we can take creative risks. When we can join in deep conversation with others, we gain ideas that spark new projects. Sharing our dreams with encouraging friends can give us clarity around our next steps. Friends even help us find opportunities, introduce us to valuable contacts, and point out elements we may have overlooked as we move through life.

GENUINE FRIENDSHIPS DISSOLVE DISTANCES

The conscientious act of nurturing friendships is a life-enhancing choice. Here is a story about a dear friend that proves this in the most extraordinary way. Through Muppet Central, a fan website, I met a young woman named Ellie Brickman. Ellie, who was a huge Muppet fan, dreamed of building puppets. She was challenged by friends and family who couldn't understand her dreams. According to Ellie, a young woman in Jerusalem didn't have a hope in the world of fulfilling such an "unrealistic" dream as this.

When Ellie reached out to me through Muppet Central, I could sense her joy and her discouragement at the same time. We eventually exchanged emails and then began speaking on the phone. She had sent me pictures of her amazing artwork and puppet builds. With a heart so genuine and a gift so great, I knew she was meant to fulfill her dreams. The year was 2007, a time of tension in Gaza between Hamas and Israel. Even though she was not near the conflict, it was still a frightening and un-predictable time for everyone who lived in the region. Still, I would continue to encourage her, fully believing she would be okay. I told her to have confidence in her dreams as a represen-tation of her destiny. Through her tears and fears I heard her heart. I knew the love and creativity within her was bigger than the negativity she faced.

When things calmed down, Ellie was able to get a flight to New York City to visit her sister, who lived in Brooklyn. I arranged to bring her to the set of *Sesame Street*; we met and it was a true celebration. She cried tears of joy about being on the set. We had so much fun. She eventually had to return to Jerusalem, but her visit to *Sesame Street* solidified her love for building puppets and brought her closer to her dreams than she could ever have imagined. We kept in close contact. Being back in the environment which brought her no hope, she receded into a state of doubting her dreams like before. To help her stay on her creative life path, I stepped up my encouragement and told her about the things from my life that I wrote in this book.

A few months went by and I got a call from Ellie. "Louis, guess where I am?" she asked.

I wasn't sure, but I took a guess. "Back in New York?"

She said she was staying in Brooklyn with her sister again and wanted me to guess where she was right at that very moment.

"Where?" I asked.

"I'm at Puppet Heap."

I was stunned by her reply.

"Guess what I'm doing?" she continued. Before I could speak, she said, "I'm sitting in front of Kermit the Frog, dressing him in a tuxedo."

Ellie had gotten an internship at Puppet Heap, the company that was hired to build and repair the Muppets after Disney acquired them and the *Bear in the Big Blue House* characters from the Jim Henson Company. While it wasn't a full-time job, she was closer than she had ever been to her Muppet dreams.

As much as this may sound like a fairytale, it's all true. Ellie's story didn't end there. After her internship ended, I received one of the most beautiful, faith-building letters I have ever read. These are Ellie's own words, punctuation and all. Thank you, Ellie, for giving me permission to share this:

More and more I see God in EVERYTHING that happens around me. And this all started with you and your encouragement. It is safe for me to say that 90% of all the good things that have happened for me in the past two years . . . have happened because I always kept what you told me in mind. You are and were my inspiration and I in return spread your message to all who are feeling low. You have changed my world. Let me explain. I never told you this because I knew that it might hurt you to hear it but my boyfriend of five years in Israel . . . was an alcoholic. I felt like the abusive and turbulent path that our relationship was on could put me in physical danger. That was when I started writing to you thinking about my dreams and my plan to start to sew the . . . puppet and collect my portfolio. Thank God I had a little financial help from my parents and was able to emotionally detach myself from the situation. It was hard for me to leave him. I felt that he needed me and that I was deserting him, his children and his ex-wife. But I knew for myself that I had to leave.

I got to New York and felt so free. Even though my working situation as you know was a little tough I still felt good to be on my own. And you were there like a beam of light telling me that I just have to keep positive. And by some stroke of luck (or God) I DID GET an internship at Puppet Heap learning how to make Muppets . . . It was incredible. I just answered a random Craig's List for a small puppet shop and that was it. After my internship was over I was a little bummed that I had to go back to the workforce and work at a children's accessory company designing accessories. BUT I learned SO much on that job. About manufacturing, pattern making and sending items for production. I then met Jonathan who is such a nice guy . . . We got married . . . Jon and I now live in Oakland California. Jon (ironically) makes wine in Napa . . . AND NOW I DESIGN PUPPETS FULL TIME AT FOLKMANIS . . . That is the kicker, Bro. EVERYTHING that I learned along the way has helped me with this job. It is both a puppet building job and a manufacturing job. JUST like you told me, Bro. I feel like I graduated from your school. I wish that everyone could have the privilege to learn from you. EVERYTHING that you told me was true and real and not just a dream . . . the naysayers had NO VOTE, Bro. I am tearing up as I write this (you know how tears come easily to me.) THANK YOU THANK YOU THANK YOU.

This story is not about my dreams. It's about the dreams born within each of us. I cannot express the joy that awaits you when you support another human's dream. The difference is that some of us listen and follow those dreams and some of us don't. Ellie came from what seemed like an impossible situation in Israel and found her true calling in life. What launched her was a little courage, a little faith, and just one voice—in this case, mine—from a tribe member, who spoke louder than the naysayers.

They didn't get a vote.

This is where I acknowledge both negative and positive people (as well as those who may be a bit of both). It is vital to recognize each human as a perpetual work in progress. This is a good thing. It is evidence of the hope and potential humanity is capable of.

DON'T FOCUS ON THE NEGATIVE

Hating humanity is a form of self-hatred. The few examples of human evil that have been sensationalized and highlighted throughout history are not proof of what we really are. There are so many examples of the greatness of love and the heights of humanity that we can reach for. But many times the media seems to live off the lowest common denominator and base human nature. Studies have shown that more people tune in to negative news. One "good news" experiment, by the online Russian newspaper *The City Reporter* brought interesting results. The paper declared to its readers that on December 1, 2014, it would publish only positive news, just for the day. After the "good news day" was over, the staff looked at their stats and found a drop of two-thirds in readership. Media companies know that bad news attracts readers and use negative news to build their audience.

Unfortunately—according to many other studies—negative news is bad for us. In one of these studies, Bryan McLaughlin,

Melissa R. Gotlieb, and Devin J. Mills, who were researchers at Texas Tech University, surveyed a national sampling of 1,100 people to learn how news (from national media outlets) affected their mental outlook. They found that 61 percent of individuals who agreed with the statement "my mind is frequently occupied with thoughts about the news," were more likely to experience negative mental, emotional, and physical symptoms than people who did not consume much or any negative news coverage. Remember the next time you read or watch the news that it is easier for media corporations to sell news that distracts us from our human greatness than it is to sell actual stories about our greatness (which, of course, is rarely mentioned at all). Protect your well-being by limiting your consumption of negative news.

The hypnotic effect news has on us can be hard to realize. Most people don't realize they've been put under a spell. News is so important to them that they will fight to stay trapped in their media-controlled hypnosis. This is why we need to turn off the news and turn toward the literature of the greatest love and the highest thinking. Regardless of your age, race, or ethnicity, you must charge yourself with the fuel of genuine life-affirming and exquisitely healthy wisdom. Otherwise you will, by osmosis, be force-fed fear and polarizing stories designed to show humanity at its worst. A constant diet of such content can transform you into a jaded, distracted, and detached human being without your awareness or permission.

Do you find yourself scrolling through pessimistic or scary news stories? Or reading negative social media posts? If you find yourself going down a bad-news rabbit hole, stop and ask yourself, what can you replace this harmful habit with?

THE CHALLENGE OF TOXIC PEOPLE

People are extremely influential and need to be identified and responded to as who they choose to be in your life. There are wonderful and beautiful people in the world. There are also seriously bad people out there. We cannot open our hearts and minds to just anyone without fully distinguishing the loving and supportive, generous and constructive, helpful and liberating people from the awful and wretched, selfish and destructive, oppressive and manipulative people. Every individual must be acknowledged as who they truly are to you and what they ultimately choose to contribute to your life. You need to be free of all damaging influences if you are to fulfill your unique life.

You will see no improvement in your life as long as you allow toxic people to infect your life; allowing these people into your world makes you an accomplice in your own creative and human dysfunction. By tolerating them—by accepting their negative treatment of you—you are partnering with them. I know this is extremely harsh, but strong words are often the only way to "hear" the importance of exiting the orbit of toxic people.

Identifying toxic people will require you to take a deeper look at your relationships. While you may not recognize a toxic person right away, you will recognize how some of their words and actions make you feel. You may find it difficult to attribute the term toxic to people who mean a lot to you. When you recognize the damage they are causing, you will realize who you may need to release from your life.

There's a difference between being "flawed" and "toxic." A habit, behavior, or action that is "flawed" is something that happens either without knowledge or real intention. It can genuinely be revealed as an "assignment." But when someone intentionally puts someone else down, deliberately targets them with cruel speech or actions, or just makes things unnecessarily difficult for anyone on purpose, they are being deliberately "toxic." Whereas a "flaw" is unintentional, toxicity is deliberate. There are some people who discover their toxicity as their "assignment" to grow from and improve upon while some others embrace their toxicity as a means of revenge or an outlet for their anger. They not only ignore their revealed assignment, they reject it and then knowingly weaponize it, especially against those who might be easily bullied.

No one has to succumb to someone who is toxic. The potential to be positive is in every human, and there is professional help if someone is not able to do it on their own. To be a loving and positive contributor to life is *always* an available choice, for everyone. But being wretched, selfish, and hateful is just as much a choice. Some people may have to undergo a tremendous amount of personal work—and perhaps get a lot of help—to shift from being a negative force to a positive one. Unfortunately, however, many negative people don't feel it is necessary to make an effort to heal. Other people enjoy inflicting misery. They prefer being miserable themselves by living out the old saying "misery loves company." By choosing to stay stuck in negativity, they are rejecting the life assignments we talked about in *Qreative Evolution.*

When people insist on being miserable, it is both rude and a waste of your precious time to wrestle this right away from them. Let them be miserable if they absolutely insist upon being so. Just don't join in and don't let them drag you into that misery.

That said, if you see them sincerely reaching for help to get out of this state of delusion, you should do whatever you genuinely and honestly can to help them. Just don't invest your time where it isn't appreciated. Individuals will reveal what kind of people they are by their behavior, words, and deeds.

"Those who don't believe in you attempt to 'protect' you *from* your process. But those who do believe in you will protect you *through* your process."
—LOUIS HENRY MITCHELL

IT BEARS REPEATING THAT THE NAYSAYERS GET NO VOTE

I've talked about naysayers elsewhere in *Qreative Evolution*, but I feel so strongly about the negative effect they can have on your life, I wanted to repeat the message here.

Throughout my youth, whenever something didn't work out in my favor, there would be naysayers at the ready to tell me how I should never have even tried. "What's wrong with you?" they'd ask. Or, "Who do you think you are?"

These put-downs always came from people who tried to convince me that I should play it safe, not reach too far, and not exhaust myself by trying to accomplish too much. Again, I celebrate my beloved mother here. Whereas the naysayers would see me trip and tell me I needed to stop being ridiculous, my mother would help me investigate why I fell, and try to help me learn from it so I might avoid falling again. Then she would encourage me to try again.

Unfortunately, sometimes the least supportive people in our lives are those who *seem* most important. Important or not, however, our feelings about a naysayer's place in our lives is no reason to allow them to continue hurting, disrupting, and destroying us. I want to make it clear that naysayers are not to be hated. I pity them because of their short-sightedness and inability to see possibilities in others or in themselves. But they are not to be tolerated on your creative journey. Sometimes you just have to be courageous enough to decide to release them, and then take the self-loving step in that direction.

> **"The naysayers do not get a vote. Ignore them and their negativity and they will eventually go away."**
> **—LOUIS HENRY MITCHELL**

THE REAL PURPOSE OF NEGATIVE PEOPLE

Many people who claim to like me have ridiculed me behind my back. You may have experienced this yourself. I usually learn of these backbiters because my dear friends want to let me know what they hear. I usually stop them, though, because it's none of my business. The backbiters are simply broken, lost, weak, and fearful people living from a sad place within themselves. They want what you have but are not strong enough to lift themselves up and work on creating it. What I hope for is that they pay enough attention to themselves and look deeper to find the tremendous potential for genuine love that is within them. Love is among the most important assignments one can discover. If you really love life and spend your time on what is good for you, you don't have time to criticize anyone else.

I share this as a reminder that negative people serve a purpose: Each is a living reminder of what you might become if you don't keep watch over yourself.

Sometimes the best way to live is in direct resistance to negative people. The way to do this is by loving them *through* their immaturity and weakness. But keep this in mind, I've also discovered that what bothers people the most (and of course I first discovered this in myself) are specific indicators of offenses they may be committing themselves. For instance, I remember criticizing some of my coworkers for borrowing pens from my desk while I wasn't there only to discover myself signing for a lunch delivery with a pen I'd never seen before. This may be somewhat humorous, but disregarding someone else's property, or, worse, their feelings is a serious issue. These people represent the warnings, self-observations, and confirmations—the inner challenges within yourself—that you need to be aware of. Will you accept the assignments revealed to you?

THE ULTIMATE TEST

Within your tribe of supportive people, you may find individuals with whom you share such a close bond that they seem like family. These people are vital to your creative life. They can give you the support to withstand challenges so large they seem insurmountable. The emotional acceptance, encouragement, motivation, and gentle pushing given by a true family member can often make the difference between fulfilling your dream or watching it die.

As you'll learn, you can discover family in myriad ways, even across continents. Love manifests between people who truly connect. It is active and evident. You don't have to coerce it from anyone. You don't even have to ask for it or question its existence when it is real. It is not difficult to see who genuinely loves and supports you. If someone claims to love you and their actions don't line up with their words, they are revealing their true feelings to you. I have learned that love doesn't become love until it is acted upon. And it is not only based on the one delivering it because love is active and it is *interactive*.

> **"Everyone says love hurts, but that is not true. Loneliness hurts. Rejection hurts. Losing someone hurts. Envy hurts. Everyone gets these things confused with love, but in reality, love is the only thing in the world that covers up all pain and makes someone feel wonderful again. Love is the only thing in this world that does not hurt."**
> **—LIAM NEESON**

If you are not vigilant, you will credit love to people from whom it does not come. In which case, you become an accomplice to your unfortunate situation, as well as an enabler of those who mask their mistreatment behind the word "love." This happens all the time, so don't think you are making a mistake if you don't immediately recognize "false love." Those who genuinely, actively, and continuously love you are your true family.

They will invest in you. They will spend their time on you. They will devote themselves to you and accept you as you are while you evolve. But there is a painfully vital truth that, if ignored, can cost you your creativity and even your very life. This truth is that there is a vital difference between family and relatives.

In my opinion, "family" lives and acts on their genuine love for you. Relatives, on the other hand, are people in your life with whom you simply share a bloodline. Unless relatives *act* like family—by living and acting on the love they profess—they are no more than blood relatives. I feel that to attribute the sacred, precious, and loving word "family" to someone just because you share blood with them is among the most self-destructive mistakes anyone can make.

"Family bonds should not be chains."
—MICHAELANTHONY ALTON MITCHELL

Family is the sacred treasure of humanity. It must be respected as such in order to earn that meaning. Family is not a matter of birth; it is a matter of revelation. Your true family is *revealed* to you. You learn and discover who your family is throughout your life. It's not a title. It's a *relationship*. This cannot be over-emphasized. When relatives act like family they *become* family. When they don't act like family, they are not family.

There are genuine tribe members who are truly family. Their actions prove their feelings for you. Some demonstrate a love so extraordinary that there is just no way to adequately put it into words. This brings me to my beloved late friend Andree' Maitland.

Two weeks before my wedding day, I'd visited Andree' Maitland's mother in the hospital. She'd had a mild heart attack but was stable enough to receive visitors. Mrs. Maitland was almost as much of a mother to me as my biological mother. The three of us—Andree', Stedroy Cleghorne, and myself—were all raised by our three mothers from adolescence to adulthood. So knowing Andree's mother was in the hospital meant that my own "mom" was in the hospital.

Andree' and I first met in 1971, the same year I discovered the comic book artist, Neal Adams, and a particularly beneficial year for me because I had discovered a great artist and obtained a great friend. Andree' was a walking encyclopedia of comic book knowledge. He knew virtually everything about every comic book, including who wrote and illustrated them. Andree' helped me on my youthful mission to collect the most obscure Neal Adams's comic book. As we grew to adulthood, Andree' and Stedroy were with me for every high and low. On my wedding day I learned just how deep Andree's love for me ran.

My wedding was planned for Thanksgiving weekend in 2004. Andree' was one of my groomsmen. It had been two weeks since I'd visited Andree's mother in the hospital. I remember telling her, "You have to get well so you can come to my wedding in two weeks." She said she would be there.

The day of the wedding was as chaotic as expected. The wedding party arrived on schedule, Andree' included. Once the ceremony ended, I finally had an opportunity to ask Andree' about his mother. "She would be here if she could," he answered. He then proceeded to laugh and party and celebrate with—and for—me.

There wasn't time for a traditional honeymoon, so my bride

and I took a brief weekend retreat together. On Monday, as I drove back home, I called Andree'. I wanted to hear how his mother was doing. "Hey, Andree'. I'm on my way home," I told him. "How's 'Mom' doing?"

Andree' said the words I was not ready to hear: "Lou, she didn't make it."

I started sobbing. When I finally regained my composure, I asked, "When did she die, Andree'?"

His answer explained it all. "Lou, I can't tell you . . ." was all he said.

I gasped. It immediately dawned on me that Mrs. Maitland had died on my wedding day. I was in shock. "But, Andree', why didn't you call me after the reception to tell me?"

Again, his answer stunned me, this time even more deeply. "Lou, she died before the wedding. At five o'clock in the morning."

I couldn't believe it. All I was able to get out of my mouth was, "But, Andree', you came. You were there . . . I asked you how she was, and you said . . ."

Then it dawned on me that he had said, "She would be here if she could."

Andree' demonstrated that he was so much more than a friend. He was a member of my tribe who cared and supported me. He was family! He partied and celebrated with me only hours after losing his own mother. I can't imagine being able to do for him what he had done for me. Andree' passed away on March 5, 2021, taking a big piece of me with him. But his gifts of love and friendship gave me so much to remember him by.

Now you know what I mean by family.

I hope that this chapter has introduced you to a new understanding of the people in your world. They can point the way to your greatness, support you when you grow weary, encourage you when you feel discouraged, and allow you to do the same for them. This is your tribe, your true family. They are the people who will help you love your way through life.

CHAPTER FIVE GUIDED SELF-EDUCATION: DISCOVERING YOUR TRIBE

Instead of the questions you've found at the end of the previous chapters, here you are going to do something a bit different: Creating your own personal *ikigai*. Before I explain what an ikigai is, I want to talk about why I am introducing it to you in a chapter based on fellowship. Being part of a tribe—a member of a creative, positive collective—is one of the most powerful gifts a human can experience. However, it may be even more important to forge a fellowship with yourself by becoming your own best friend. As I mentioned earlier, you need to become a student of yourself in order to intentionally create your life. This entails learning what motivates you and what you truly feel you are here for. The ikigai will help with this. As we've explored in this chapter, how you live your life influences both how you appear to yourself and who appears in your life. Seeing that your life and your tribe are intimately connected, it is worth genuinely examining your own life. An ikigai can help you see your life in a deeper way.

An ikigai is a tool that I was introduced to through a mentoring program in which I had one mentee for eight months.

(I learned from my years of teaching that teachers usually learn more from a class than the actual students. A teacher goes into a classroom with his own thoughts and plans, which the students beautifully disrupt. The teacher must then rise to the occasion of guiding the students toward the fulfillment of their purpose in the class, and often also in life.) According to the *World History Encyclopedia*, ikigai originated during Japan's Heian Period, which started from 794 to 1185 AD and is "a Japanese concept referring to something that gives a person a sense of purpose, a reason for living." It consists of four overlapping circles (passion, mission, vocation, and profession) in which eight of the divisions are filled with the following topics:

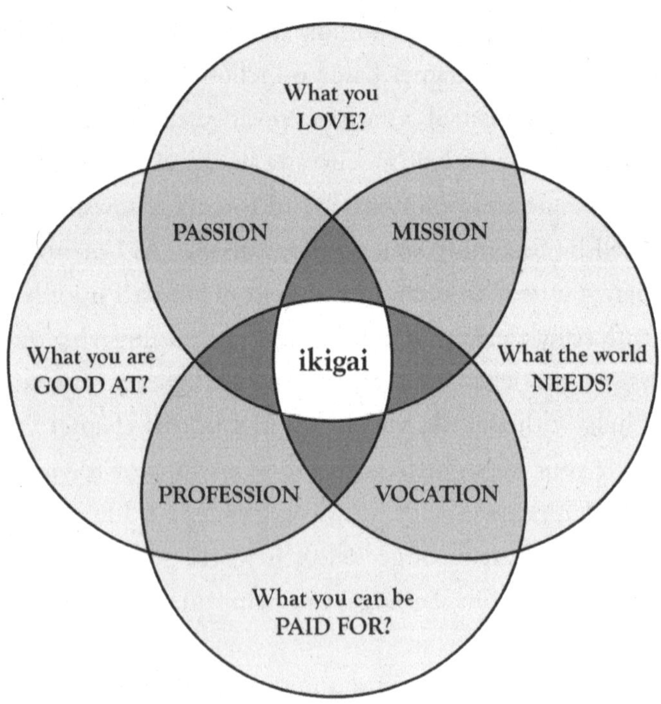

I made my own ikigai diagram unique to my calling:

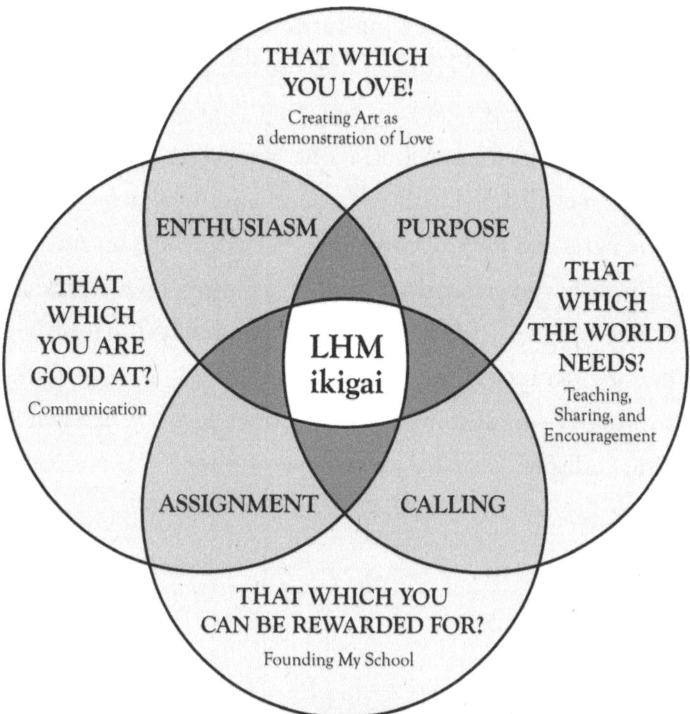

First, I replaced "Passion" with "Enthusiasm" and wrote "Creating Art as Demonstration of Love" under "that which you love."

Then I replaced "Mission" with "Purpose" and wrote "Teaching, Sharing, and Encouragement" under "that which the world needs."

Next I replaced "Vocation" with "Calling" and wrote "Founding My School" under "that which you can be rewarded for."

Finally, I replaced "Profession" with "Assignment" and wrote "Communication" under "that which you are good at."

The focus and clarity of the ikigai serves as a compass for me. It's a very quick reference that charges me and helps me stay on target. Many times as I put forth my best efforts, or simply get caught up in the chaos of life, the ikigai is a jolt of energy that reminds me of who I am and what I am seeking to accomplish. I may pick it up to look at one specific part depending on what I am challenged with at the moment. Inevitably, I look at all the parts and they all come together as a whole for me. And because I have personalized mine, it is in my own words and hits my inner target that much more accurately. It has become a literary member of my tribe.

Now it's your turn to make your own ikigai. When you are finished, display it where you will see it often.

Chapter Six

TRANSCENDENT QREATIVITY

Transcendent. As I thought about a word to express the *Qreative Evolution* experience as a whole, this is the word that came to mind. It describes something that crosses or goes beyond the limits of ordinary experience. It can also mean a thing that is far better or greater than what is usual. Synonyms of transcendent include unparalleled, extraordinary, superior. When I think back on my life's journey from childhood to where I am now, I can say without question that it has been transcendent.

In my wildest dreams I couldn't have imagined many of my life's most treasured moments. I now realize, however, that these experiences did not occur randomly. They happened because I followed my heart. It refused to listen to my doubts or the naysayers around me; it focused only on my desires, which led me to my dreams. If you've wondered why you are here or what you are meant to accomplish during your lifetime, here is the powerfully simple answer: You are here to *create your life . . . on purpose*. With intent.

To help you see the connection between your desires and

your life, I want to share a special story with you. It is one of the greatest—and most unexpected—validations of my entire life. As you read it, I hope you will think of your own life and see past the barriers you may have created around your desires.

> **THE WORLD NEEDS YOU TO BE YOU**
>
> You may encounter people who want you to live a replica of *their* lives. They want you to have their experiences, replicate their outcomes, develop their abilities, follow their dreams. Why? When everyone follows the same life path, everyone gets pretty much the same results. No one outshines anyone else. No one stands out. Everyone's the same. No one feels compelled to work harder or think differently or take uncomfortable risks. Unfortunately for anyone who wants us all to be the same, the world needs you to be who you really are.

I HAVE A DREAM . . . AND IT CAME TRUE

Anything you feel inspired to do should be pursued with enthusiasm and your deepest love. This activity you have thrown yourself into may not ultimately be something you continue on with. And that's okay. There are lessons and knowledge and opportunities that come from that pursuit that will guide you to your next level. "Completing" a particular desire may not be the actual purpose of the pursuit. There may be something—or someone—you need that may be available only through fully engaging with that desire. This story exemplifies this.

I consider Dr. Martin Luther King Jr. to be one of my greatest mentors. Though I did not have the opportunity to meet him before he died in 1968, his impact on my life is immeasurable and I often seek his wisdom. While former president Ronald Reagan signed legislation in 1983 making Martin Luther King Jr. Day a federal holiday, the first actual observance of the day didn't occur until 1986. In 1985 I felt inspired to help promote this official holiday. Dr. King was especially devoted to children and I thought that the public schools of our nation should hold a special commemoration of this important holiday on the first day of its celebration on January 20, 1986.

At the time, I was the first Black art director at McCaffrey & McCall Advertising in New York City. I approached the agency's senior creative director, Royal Bruce Montgomery, for support in running an educational campaign in the nation's public schools. I hoped to present my idea to the Martin Luther King Jr. Center for Nonviolent Social Change. Bruce—the name Mr. Montgomery was known by—arranged for our agency to book a flight to the center's headquarters in Atlanta, Georgia, once I had an appointment with key people there. One of my desires was that the agency would pay for the entire campaign, which included a booklet highlighting Dr. King's childhood, another booklet highlighting his adult life, and a series of three posters that I would design and illustrate.

When I arrived at the center I was escorted to a waiting area where I was eventually met by Mrs. Christine King Farris, Dr. King's sister. That alone was amazing to me. I did not expect to meet anyone from Dr. King's family. After I presented my campaign to her and her husband, she said something I could not believe: "Oh, Coretta has to see this." She wanted me to present the campaign to Dr. King's wife Coretta Scott King. I agreed, though I did not honestly believe it was going to happen. Mrs. King's assistant entered and asked if I could keep my presentation to two minutes due to the fact that Mrs. King had a cold. I said I could do it in one minute if that would be more helpful. Her assistant agreed. (I still, however, didn't believe it was going to happen.)

Mrs. King's assistant escorted me to an office. There she was: Mrs. Coretta Scott King herself. She had a little sniffle but that did not minimize her astounding beauty. I said hello and introduced myself. I was intimidated but so elated.

She looked at me and said, "Hello, Louis. What do you have to show me?"

I showed her designs and drawings and explained every part of the campaign to her. She listened intently with a look of great interest. After I concluded, she looked me in the eye and said in a very serious tone, "Okay, young man. How much is this all going to cost me?"

I told her that the advertising agency I worked for had its own printing plant and would be paying for the printing and distribution. All I needed from her was her blessing.

Mrs. King seemed shocked. "You mean you didn't come here to ask me for anything but my blessing?"

I explained to her that with all that she and Dr. King had done for the world, what could I possibly ask from her except her blessing as I attempted to celebrate their work and Dr. King's life? She was delighted. She told me that I was the first person who had come to her wanting nothing but her blessing. She then turned to her assistant. "Give this young man anything he needs," she proclaimed.

The surprising end of this story was due to circumstances

beyond my control. I was prevented from completing this assign-ment. I was not able to get messages to Mrs. King anymore and the people I was working with seemed to be too overwhelmed with their own work to give me the attention I needed. Many years passed before I understood the meaning behind what I had experienced. Even though the campaign did not happen, I did get to meet Coretta Scott King, the wife of my great hero and indirect mentor, Dr. Martin Luther King Jr. This is the climax of this story. The very reason I was allowed to meet her became apparent when I showed her the drawings I had done of Dr. King for the posters. She looked at them long and hard and then, looking me straight in the eyes, she said, "Young man, these are the greatest drawings of my husband I have ever seen."

Those words still ring loudly in both my mind and heart, validating my path as an artist. I realized *that* was the reason I acquired access to her: to be reinforced on my path as an artist who would be placed before great people. The purpose of meet-ing her was to receive validation of my talent from Mrs. Coretta Scott King herself. Despite the fact that the project I wanted to create did not happen, I followed my heart and it led me to one of the greatest people I have ever met.

"A man's gift makes room for him, and brings him before great men."

—PROVERBS 18:16

TRANSCENDENT QREATIVITY

I must admit that this is the chapter I have been looking for-ward to sharing the most. This is where we bring everything together and then expand the learnings beyond what we have already discussed. You've come this far, and your launchpad has been built for such a time as this. Here we enter the fullness of *Qreative Evolution* through its most potent dimension: Transcendent Qreativity.

> **YOUR NEXT LEVEL**
>
> Whenever you experience a challenging emotion—such as fear, frustration, or anger—you now know you are being given an assignment. When a challenge shows up, life is offering you the next opportunity for your development. It's like you've completed one level of your life and have received the assignment that will allow you to graduate to the next. Learn to recognize your assignments. Replace the torment of seeing "flaws" with the joy of acknowledging you are being entrusted with your next step.

YOUR MORNING OF VICTORY

Prepare for each day with a morning of victory. Research has shown that how we begin our morning can influence our entire day. A 2011 study conducted by the National Sleep Foundation (NSF) concluded that individuals who make their beds every day are 19 percent more likely to get a good night's sleep compared to those who leave their beds unmade. The study also found a connection between making your bed and higher happiness and productivity levels. The NSF ran a survey in 2018 that found that 71 percent of bed makers claim to be happy with their lives, while 62 percent of non-bed-makers admit to being unhappy. It's been said that simply making your bed in the morning is about far more than just keeping a tidy bedroom. It offers you an early victory. Your first positive accomplishment of the day imbues you with the invincible feeling of success, which then motivates you to carry that powerful feeling with you through your entire day. Some of us are able to do this as a habit, but there are other areas in life where the same kind of victory doesn't occur, like keeping an organized workspace or clothing closet. That morning victory can lead you to perpetuate it in other areas of your life. So, starting with making the bed, you can be consciously aware of other opportunities in which to be victorious. Making the bed could serve as an achievable daily launchpad to many other things.

According to behavioral science, our willpower is strongest in the morning, meaning this time is a gift we can use to accomplish what is important to us. The reason for high morning willpower isn't exactly known, but researchers think it may be that most people are rested, alert, and haven't yet faced demands on their time.

I focus on music and art as my early victories in the morning. After I get dressed, I sit at my drawing table, pull up an inspiring audio recording to listen to, choose something I intend to draw for my daily practice, and then begin. After I have taken the drawing to a good place, I stop. I will consider it finished or plan to continue working on it over the next few mornings. I then move to my piano and play whatever comes into my heart, be it improvisational or most likely one of the pieces that I am working on. By the time I've completed this personal morning routine, my spirit, mind, and body will be ignited and aligned with my life's purpose. The flow of creative energy in those early morning hours is a gift I give to myself every day. What about you? How could you use your mornings to ignite your creativity and align with your goals?

PAUSED: FROZEN IN PLACE

Unfortunately, not everyone keeps moving forward. Some people freeze where they are and never make any genuine progress. They ignore their assignments and stop listening to the calling of their desires. If you don't do your assignments, you're still not flawed—we are never flawed—but you *are* paused (or *frozen*). The problem with being frozen is that the feeling of stagnation can deeply affect you. It can leave you feeling stressed, anxious, and lacking in integrity. It also slows your personal development and affects your self-esteem. The good news is that an assignment is always waiting for you. You can take yourself off pause and begin an assignment, thereby fulfilling your lesson and moving toward victory.

THE REVERSED WORD "LOVE"

This is a great opportunity to explain *Qreative Evolution*'s logo. I was meditating on *Qreative Evolution*'s content and what it means to me. When I looked at the first four letters of "evolution" I saw "love" spelled backward, I was moved to keep these letters reversed as a sign. Take the logo and hold it up to a mirror. When you are looking at the word love in reverse, you'll see that love is being directed outward *from* you *to* others.

"How you love yourself is how you teach others to love you."

—RUPI KAUR

I think of this as a reminder that you are the source of love. That love starts with you before it is shown to anyone else. It emanates from you. Self-love, the love that fuels all other loves, is not a place where you arrive. It's a journey. It can take some time to get there as it's something that's cultivated constantly over your entire lifetime. Self-love is not selfishness. It involves establishing a healthy relationship with yourself. Be kind to yourself. Love yourself. Be the love you want to see and experience in this world. What do you think it means to love yourself? What does loving yourself look like? If you need some help, start by thinking about how it feels when you love someone. Can you love yourself the same way you love them?

"Loving yourself isn't vanity; it's sanity."
—KATRINA MAYER

WHAT DOES IT MEAN TO TRULY LOVE YOUR LIFE?

As I've said throughout *Qreative Evolution*, you create your own life with every action you take. Your life is your own most precious creation. To love your life doesn't only mean to enjoy it. It means to love it by protecting it, nurturing it, and cultivating it. Don't let those who don't mean well engage with your life, and avoid allowing others to influence or shape it. Creating your life is your responsibility alone. Honor your life with healthy living, positive experiences, supportive people, and the knowledge that you alone are responsible for creating it.

To love your life is to do those things and more

> because it's *your* life. The enjoyment of life is the
> by-product of loving it.

**"Don't change so people will like you. Be yourself
and the right people will love the real you."**
—SABRINA CADINI

THE PURPOSE OF INTEGRITY

It is vital to keep the promises we make to ourselves, so that the promises made to others will also have genuine value. The ability to honor one's word is evidence of integrity, a word that means moral uprightness, the quality of being honest, and having strong moral principles. People with integrity do what they say they will. They hold themselves to high standards.

Integrity is vital to humanity and it is vital to the creation of your best life. It is true that many people live outside of integrity, either unintentionally or from a place of negativity. Watch for them and limit your interactions with them, but know that integrity ultimately benefits you. You need to know that you are trustworthy and willing to be your best for yourself. You need to know that even if no one else is watching you would do the right thing. This is how you learn to trust yourself.

Avoid doing things that compromise your integrity with yourself, your thoughtlife, and your private life. Integrity is not about trying to be perfect. It's knowing that even in your errors, you seek to correct, repair, and restore what you may be responsible for doing wrong.

Ignoring your personal integrity can numb you to the call of your life and the direction of your heart. Because we are such powerful beings, we can shift gears inwardly based upon what we focus and concentrate on. This can go either way, for your benefit or to your detriment. Why not be deliberate about this powerful endowment and use your personal integrity to move you in the right direction?

WHY ARE YOU HERE?

What do you believe you are here for? You are here to create yourself. You are your primary assignment. When you approach any assignment, it is imperative to avoid any negative motivation. A person may stand up for something important but be motivated in a destructive way. Here's an example. Someone is an avid animal activist trying to expose the malicious treatment of animals raised for fur. They can protest and bring attention to their cause with signs and social media messages and by reaching out to politicians, writing articles, and creating educational curricula around animal cruelty. But they could also become destructive by defacing property or attacking people by throwing blood at them. Their first course of action could have a tremendous impact by helping draw attention to the victims of this cruel industry. But their second course of action could divert attention from their cause by overshadowing it with destruction and negativity (and could get them arrested!).

Don't stop at what you hate. Keep going until you discover that what you hate is ultimately revealing what you love if you take your thoughtlife far enough. Remember, emotions are indicators. They are not meant to be motivators. They are meant to reveal where you are at any given moment so you can *respond* rather than *react* to whatever you may be facing.

Find motivation through benevolence rather than malevolence. When you recognize what looks like a flaw as an assignment, you are recognizing a purpose and specific meaning of your life. I keep going back to this because it is vital. When you discover an area in your life that needs work, it doesn't mean you are flawed. It means you are ready to rise to a higher level on your life's journey.

MAKING TIME FOR LIFE

Similar to how paint can be mixed and clay formed, time is a *medium*. When you commit to deliberately creating your life, you don't *find* time, you *make* time. How you decide to use your time indicates the level of your commitment. Many people unthinkingly use the phrase "make time" without realizing the power of it. Time is far more than that.

Time is part of you. It's embedded in your creativity. It is an element of the life you are living. I know this may sound esoteric, but let me explain. I'm frequently asked how I'm able to do so many different things—such as writing music, building puppets, drawing daily, writing a book, and supporting mentees and students, among other things—while working full-time for *Sesame Street*. My answer is that I respect time by doing what has been revealed to me as my calling. I have discovered that when you are doing what you are truly supposed to be doing, and what's in line with what's been revealed to you for your life, there is more than enough time. It's when you are wasting your time on things that don't contribute to your growth and that don't serve the purpose of your life that you feel overwhelmed and realize there isn't enough time for those things. This is why examining your desires is important *before* committing to an activity.

"Work expands so as to fill the time available for its completion."

—C. NORTHCOTE PARKINSON

There is more to life than meets the eye. As you move in the direction of your life's purpose, time will gift itself to you in almost miraculous ways according to your dedication to what you know you need to be doing. Of course you will face challenges. Building your best life requires that you overcome obstacles, both those inside and outside of you. This is an opportunity to let go of those time-stealing activities that do not contribute positively to your life, and become clear on the activities that will help you create your life.

What time-stealers are you facing now that you can adjust or eliminate? Your present life is the direct result of your past decisions. It's time to start discovering the direction of your life as you follow your heart. Your decisions won't interfere with what will be revealed to you. What new discoveries will you find today to influence your tomorrow, and even the rest of your life?

"Rise above just the skill."

—ANNETTE AUGERI

A REMINDER ABOUT HUMANITY

Some of the most life-changing lessons I have received are about our human condition and our responses to being human. The reason I can be so positive about humanity is because I fully acknowledge its negative side. It is vital to embrace the love and joy in life while simultaneously acknowledging the pain and suffering—and even the evil—that humans are capable of. But there is a difference between embracing and acknowledging. I believe embracing is becoming deeply intimate with and accepting what you are taking in—even reciprocating with it. Embracing humanity's dark side will not help you. What will help you is acknowledging, which is being aware of what is happening around you so you can maneuver around it or navigate through it.

As I move through a work project with other people, I like to openly express the joy I am experiencing. There may be someone, however, who doesn't appreciate my joy and who may even verbally attack it. I have even been called "irritating" because of the joy I discover from a challenging project, or even life, itself. This always brings me back to the purpose of negative people. By not doing their "homework" and fulfilling their assignments, they aren't able to see the benefits and blessings of being employed. All of us can decide to look through a positive lens and see challenges, such as time-intensive work projects, as lessons or training rather than burdens or inconveniences. I find that as I retain my positive approach and even remind people of the benefits of a project, they are able to see the gifts contained in the work. By standing my ground in the face of negativity, I can help others see differently. This also strengthens my own commitment to positivity.

One other very significant purpose negative people play is to reveal what can happen to you if you don't respect and accept your assignments when they've been revealed to you.

> How can you retain a positive approach as you
> face challenging situations? When you stop
> thinking how hard it is—or even how easy it is—
> and focus on just on what you need to do, you'll
> find your creativity expanding.

"It is of no use saying, 'We are doing our best.' You have got to succeed in doing what is necessary."
—WINSTON CHURCHILL

"Those who are *against* you are revealed by fearfully 'protecting' you *from* your life's processes. Those who are *for* you are revealed by lovingly supporting you *through* your life's processes."
—LOUIS HENRY MITCHELL

This is why it is vital to live honestly and with genuine integrity. Help appears when you actively follow your heart and your dreams. As you live out your process fully and on purpose, mentors, supporters, and champions will be revealed. Likewise, as soon as you begin living your purpose, naysayers and enemies will be exposed and then repelled.

What does this mean? People who can't stand individuals who are "too happy" will find all kinds of ways to avoid them. And that is their gift to you. As these people are revealed, keep a grudgeless vigil toward them. They have chosen who they want to be in your life.

One of the greatest "people filters" in my life is my feelings about the days of the week. I don't play favorites. I don't enjoy Saturdays any more than I enjoy Mondays. In fact, I adore

Mondays. They represent a fresh start to me. Just watch how passionless people, or those too jaded to appreciate each and every day as a gift, will moan and groan (and even run from you) when you learn to love and appreciate each and every day equally, Mondays included. It becomes very cleansing. You want to attract the people who, even when times are bad, don't lose sight of the blessing of life. They don't forget the potential of every challenging moment to become a blessing. If you want success in your life (based on what success means to you), identify those who love life and those who fear it. Then respond accordingly.

LOOKING *THROUGH* THE CLICHÉS

A cliché is a phrase that was once taken as truth, but with time has become so overused, that it has lost its power to teach a lesson. I mention clichés because phrases we hear frequently can influence our thoughtlives. Here is a short list of clichés I personally avoid:

"Think outside of the box." We create the box that we believe we are thinking outside of. In other words, the only way to be caught in a box is by creating it. When you stop believing in "the box," you are free from the imaginary friction, resistance, and distraction of believing there are specific boundaries you are trapped inside of. Remember, *there is no box.*

"Live every day as if it were your last." This has always sounded fatalistic to me. Why think in terms of loss and limits? Every day is a fresh start, a gift that allows you to acknowledge and enjoy your talents, your gifts, your tribe, and your life. Children never think about their last day. They wake up anticipating what will happen that day. We can do the same. Imagine living your life from a place of anticipation.

"Life is what happens to you while you're busy making other plans." Now that you've reached the last chapter of *Qreative Evolution*, you know my belief on life, and how your life is created. So it probably is no surprise that I do not agree with this cliché. Life doesn't just happen to you—not if you are an active participant. In *Qreative Evolution*, you purposefully create your life, moment by moment. Life is your creation, not something that arbitrarily "just happens to you."

"Shoot for the moon. Even if you miss, you'll land among the stars." We've been to the moon. We can see the sun. Of course, this is all figurative, but why not aim further, to a place where you cannot see or even anticipate? Let your reach exceed your grasp. That's where the surprises are and where the potential lies for creating what may have never yet been seen. It's true that "there is nothing new under the sun." So, let's explore far beyond it. If we aim beyond what we think is possible, we will find something new. Shoot beyond the sun!

"If life gives you lemons, make lemonade." What if all you have is a lemon? Yes, make the lemonade and enjoy it (or sell it), but save the seeds for planting so you can grow an orchard to multiply the lemons you were given by life. This can translate into a humble opportunity being made into a Fortune 500 company. Whatever you have can be made into something far more valuable than what it looks like on the surface. Reach further. Dig deeper.

"The best things in life are free." While not everything costs money, nothing is free. Everyone pays for everything they receive (if not with money, then with time or effort). And, really, it shouldn't be any other way. Paying (again, not always with money) shows commitment. It's the only way to harvest the benefits of life. I love to play the piano. I love to draw. I love to pose the *Sesame Street* Muppets for photoshoots. They all came at a great cost of working hard and trying to get as good at doing them as I could, which I still work toward. So, nothing is truly free and, honestly, I don't want things to be free. There is wisdom to gain and commitment to show when you pay for the things in life.

"If it ain't broke don't fix it." Where is the room for improvement in that statement? Where is the creativity, the evolution? We should always be seeking to have better resources, do better, become better.

"No pain no gain." This phrase came from the sport of bodybuilding and it has its place there. But people often apply it to many of the necessary tasks in their lives they don't want to do. I've even heard the saying applied to getting out of bed. Referring to daily activities as "painful" reinforces the idea that waking up and launching into life is something to dread. I was there once. But when I started seeing what I could accomplish by launching into my day, I stopped associating daily activities with pain, and replaced my old negativity with excitement. Getting to "work" at *Sesame Street* was a dream come true. I didn't have to be in until 9:30 a.m. But I was at my desk by 7:30 a.m. every morning from the day I started. So many people told me it would wear off in a few months. What started in 1992 and became full-time in 2000 continues to this day. Sometimes even earlier. I feel no pain whatsoever in getting up, most times before the alarm clock goes off, to go into Manhattan and meet up with Cookie Monster and other friends.

"Get out of your comfort zone." This common platitude is among the most distracting and misused of these clichés. While it is important to step out of your comfort zone to learn and grow in truly amazing ways from time to time, no one is meant to stay perpetually outside of their comfort zone. After an intense session or season outside of the comfort zone, it is necessary to reenter it to reflect and replenish in true comfort. Your comfort zone is where you recover and process what you've learned outside of it. This is something I never hear when people encourage us to leave our comfort zones. Go back in and refresh before the next session outside of your comfort zone.

"There are no such things as limits to growth, because there are no limits on the human capacity for intelligence, imagination, and wonder."
—RONALD REAGAN

CHALLENGE YOURSELF. ALWAYS.

We are made to overcome challenges. Our reward for facing something difficult is growth. A 2018 LinkedIn survey of 2,049 business professionals from various fields showed that individuals who engaged in some kind of learning for five or more hours per week were more likely to be "happier, less stressed, more productive, confident, and more ready to grow." Researchers at Duke University asked 120 undergrad students to undergo simple memory-based math problems to stimulate a portion of their prefrontal cortex, while they underwent a noninvasive brain scan to access brain activity. The results indicated that challenging oneself may stimulate brain function, reduce anxiety and depression, and has a number of other benefits, including increased focus, self-esteem, happiness, and motivation. My own experience with challenging myself mirrors this.

Facing challenges is in your DNA. It's a part of your ancient wisdom. Modern conveniences can make us comfortable, but they will not make us creative. Creativity comes when you challenge yourself with tasks and situations that seem new and difficult but will lead to great growth. What challenges have you faced that you have overcome? What did you learn from those challenges that you can apply to your life? What *new* challenges can you invite into your life to help you grow even further?

FOCUS AND THE GIFT OF SILENCE

We touched on silence earlier in *Qreative Evolution*. But we will immerse deeper here. Quiet time is an ancient gift that is a necessary part of the human condition. Silence may help decrease stress by lowering cortisol levels, which in turn lowers anxiety, increases brain function, improves concentration, decreases blood pressure, stimulates brain growth, encourages mindfulness, and boosts creativity.

However, silence is often sacrificed in the twenty-first century to traffic and ambulances, car stereos, lawnmowers, power tools, household appliances, video games, and whatever it is we are listening to (with or without our headphones). The constant noise that surrounds us can leave us feeling anxious, raise our blood pressure, cause headaches, and distract us.

Of course, we should enjoy music, conversations, walking down city sidewalks, and using our appliances. These things—and many other activities that involve sound—make life more enjoyable and help us learn how to live. But at some point, we need to process all these sounds. Silence removes the competition for your brain's attention so it can focus deeply on your thoughts, ideas, and creations. Silence also lets you work and create efficiently by removing the sounds that can divert your focus.

I want to share a story about how I accidentally discovered the gifts that come from quiet. When the first Sony Walkman tape cassette player came out, it was the beginning of our relinquishment of personal silence. Don't get me wrong. I loved my Walkman and took it everywhere. I remember going on a long bus trip to Moorestown, New Jersey, from New York City, to visit my girlfriend. I was well-prepared for the nearly two-hour ride with fresh batteries and a collection of my favorite cassette tapes . . . or so I thought.

It wasn't until I had fully settled into my bus seat and we had begun our lengthy journey that I reached into my backpack for my Walkman. It wasn't there. I realized that I had forgotten to pack it. I even contemplated asking the driver to let me off so I could go home to get it. The frustration I felt at forgetting my Walkman was indescribable. I didn't want to draw or read or daydream. I just wanted my Walkman. Even though the trip was a visit to my girlfriend, all I could think about was that I had no music for the trip.

But something happened about an hour into the trip. My mind began to wander. Without effort or even realizing it, I was exploring my dreams, the things I was hoping for in my life. I remembered when my friend Andree' and I went to see *Star Wars* on the very first day it came out. I remembered some of my favorite moments on *The Muppet Show*. I even relived the beautiful anxiety of trying to copy the face of the old man looking up at the speaker in Norman Rockwell's painting *Freedom of Speech* from his Four Freedoms series. Some music I'd been learning to play on the piano was also running through my mind, followed by memories of things my mother and I had done together.

Before I knew it, my sketchpad and notebook were out and I was drawing, writing, and *thinking* in ways I hadn't in a long time. And the only music I had was the muffled hum of the moving bus wheels and the occasional whisper of wind. I was alone with my thoughts on an uncrowded bus, with the empty seat beside me as my studio.

I was nineteen years old when this happened and it taught me a lesson that resonates even more today: Creativity thrives in silence. The very ideas I share in this book grew and were harvested in quiet. Silence has helped humanity create our way to where we are now.

We live in a distracting world. Cultivating silence is a tremendous challenge both inwardly and outwardly. Are you willing to do what's necessary to fulfill your creative calling and life purpose? Silence lets you find yourself. Commit to the creative power of silence. Build quiet time into your day. Start your morning in a tranquil way, without the television or radio playing. Instead of wearing headphones on your daily walk, focus on the world around you. At night, try falling asleep to a book, or an online audio of an eight-hour gentle rainfall, instead of the nighttime news or any music. You will soon find yourself feeling calmer, as well as more focused, productive and creative. Quiet time just might be among the most important parts of your day. This takes time to cultivate if you don't do it, but the rewards are indescribable.

If you feel that you don't have enough quiet time in your day, what could you do to create more? What would you have to do to experience tranquility in your life? What time of day would be best for you to have peaceful moments and how could you schedule that in?

"The maturity of a man—that means to have reacquired the seriousness that one had as a child at play."
—FRIEDRICH NIETZSCHE

BE AS A CHILD

Throughout *Qreative* Evolution, I have shared personal stories that were meant to show you joy and freedom. Now would be a great time to reflect on your own childhood and discover your own stories that can remind you of who you really are deep inside—the inner child with great dreams of the future. Who are among the most carefree people you see in life? Children. Look back at your childhood. What did you love to do? Were there activities or items you were particularly focused on? Do you remember the sense of fearlessness you felt, like you could do anything? What made you happy? What did you dream for yourself? What did you love?

Think back on your favorite games and activities and toys. Maybe it was a teddy bear who somehow understood everything you went through, or a special coin that commemorates a very unique moment of joy, or a pencil you always loved to use when you wrote things down. These are early clues to your calling, your purpose. Retrieve a favorite toy that brought you pleasure and comfort and that stimulated your imagination. Keep these things close and easily visible to remind you of your childlike self, the *real* you. They can unleash a flood of memories of key moments in your development, a time when you were learning how wonderful you were.

Here is another powerful way to keep your childhood wisdom alive: Find a photo from your childhood—preferably before the age of ten years old—when you were becoming aware of who you are. Place this picture in a prominent place. The young person in that photo is your greatest mentor. He or she will remind you of who you *really* are. I keep a picture of six-year-old Louis Henry Mitchell on my desk at work, and another one in my home studio. I was six years old when I first saw Jim Henson on *The Ed Sullivan Show* carrying Kermit the Frog. I talked about this memory at the beginning of *Qreative Evolution*. It was the moment when I started becoming the Louis Henry Mitchell I am today.

"Genius is the recovery of childhood at will."
—ARTHUR RIMBAUD

It may take some real effort on your part to find clues to help you rediscover yourself. It can also be difficult for those who may have had particularly difficult childhoods. But because children tend to find a way to keep playing, even in the midst of challenging and difficult times, I believe delight, joy and excitement can still be revealed to them. It is worth rediscovering those wonderful childhood moments for yourself.

Please take the time to do this. Find childhood artifacts—like favorite toys or books you loved—that revealed the true you, moments when you felt a creative fire and realized your creative greatness. You can revisit the creative awareness you experienced in childhood anytime you need a reminder of who you are and what your purpose is.

Once again, your childhood self is your greatest mentor.

THE IMPORTANCE OF PLAY

What is the single most spectacular trait of being a child? Playfulness. Play is serious business to children. Playtime is when children learn to be fair, to socialize, and to learn about helpful rules that keep everyone playing the same game when called for. But play is also one of the greatest ways children learn how to be creative, and how to exercise their personal freedom.

Children are the embodiment of faith and immense potential. They are vulnerable, so they need guidance and protection as they are raised. But children are filled with a capacity for wisdom, faith, and trust beyond explanation. As we grow from children into teenagers and then adults, some of us are robbed of our early promise, through illness, abuse, neglect, and other negative states. We can, however, rediscover our true selves and find out who we were as children. Start with play.

Your own inner child wants and needs engagement regularly. Find ways to have fun, with your tribe and by yourself. Think back to what you loved to do when you were a child, and do it again now. Try new things that interest you. Create something. Learn something. Enjoy yourself. You must continue to play in order to keep alive the essence of who you are.

CHILDREN CAN BE THE GREATEST TEACHERS

What you can learn from rediscovering your childhood self can be found in how we can learn from other children. Danson Mandela Wambua has become one of the greatest teachers of my life. This young man—who was seven years old when he wrote the book, *Danson: The Extraordinary*

*Discovery of an Autistic Child's Innermost Thoughts
and Feelings*—is wiser than many adults I know.
This is one of those landmark books that helped me
understand my own inner life. Here is one gem of
wisdom from his book, which he wrote through his
beautiful mother, Michele Pierce Burns. It is small
and powerful, and has influenced me a great deal:
"Live your life like you mean it."

To me Danson's quote is a reminder to
enjoy every moment of my creative life while
simultaneously gifting it to others, without seeing a
line dividing those two actions. This idea was given
to me by a child with autism who is tapped into life
in the most extraordinary way. We were all once
tapped into our inner lives when we were children.
Maybe not in the same way as Danson, but we
were certainly tapped in. If you have forgotten who
you are, you can remember by returning to the
powerful greatness of childhood.

DO WHAT YOU *HATE* LIKE YOU *LOVE* IT

I was watching an interview with Mike Tyson, the famous boxer
and youngest heavyweight boxing champion in history. The in-
terviewer asked Tyson how he had successfully won so many
championships. Tyson explained in detail the level and intensity
of the training he endured in order to keep getting better and
better at his sport. To interpret his experience as merely difficult would diminish the hours, days, weeks, and months it took
him to prepare for his bouts, not to mention the diet he had to

follow. You could tell he truly did not enjoy everything he had to do, but knew he had to do it in order to be his very best. As he put it, "Do what you hate like you love it!"

I was astounded. In relation to the life of extreme discipline that was evident in his life, his comment made perfect sense. However, as with all things that move me, I needed to personalize it. I took Tyson's comment and used it as a launchpad for my own mantra. Filtering his quote through the *Qreative Evolution* lens, I realized the part that was missing for me. This is how I made Tyson's quote my own: "Do what you hate like you love it . . . until you *do* love it!"

Mike Tyson's phrase resonated with me so much because it was something I held in my heart even before I heard it. But the saying felt negative until I added "until you *do* love it" to infuse the phrase with hope and potential. We are creatures of habit. We are also extremely adaptable—even to extreme or negative things. Instead of succumbing to habits that might be detrimental to us, we can use this superpower to our advantage and deliberately create habits that empower us. A good thing we've learned to hate, like daily exercise, can be shifted in our thoughtlife when we learn to do it as if we loved it. How many people hate running until they eventually realize they can't live without their early morning run, rain or shine?

Over time you will cultivate an appreciation (and love) for the positive activities you commit to that may have been unpleasant to you, even though they are good for you. Through the course of committing to something habitually, it will gradually become a part of you that you will miss if you don't do it. When you know something that is good for you but you hate it, start training yourself to appreciate it in your thoughtlife. Tell yourself that you love it and act as if you love it. Literally say out loud that you love what you are doing and how it is helping you be the best you can be. Hearing yourself say something aloud, in your own voice, with conviction, can anchor the sentiment in your soul. Writing an affirmation for this can also work, like using a sculpting tool to reshape resistance so you can forge an appreciation for that which is great but that you initially hate. Eventually, as you stay committed to the activity, your love for it will become a genuine part of you.

The best example I can give from my own life is exercise. This was something I really didn't enjoy doing, but I knew it would help me feel healthier. When I thought about the best time to fit exercise into my day, the morning made the most sense for me, because the days become more complex and demanding as they move along. The challenge I faced, however, was in using my precious morning hours on something I didn't love. I am an early bird, but I didn't want to use my early hours for exercise. I preferred to start my day with meditating, drawing, and playing the piano.

However, once I began telling myself that I loved exercising in the morning and reminded myself how it would help me meet my goal of being healthier, my attitude toward exercise changed. I began bounding out of bed early, looking forward to my morning rituals, which now includes exercise.

Are there activities that you know would be good for you, but that you dislike and avoid doing?

What can you do to change the way you think about them, so you are willing to fit them into your life? Is there an affirmation that can help you see the activity in a new, positive way—or an affirmation that you can adjust to make your own?

NOT AVOIDANCE BUT *FOCUS*

Focus on the positive results that you want, rather than wasting your energy avoiding what you don't want. The power behind this is that you can work virtually any beneficial behavior into your life with committed practice. As a reminder, you can use your time to make subtle *or* significant adjustments to your life, simply by applying action and patience to any worthwhile endeavor. It's important to note that many subtle changes can add up to create a significant breakthrough without you even realizing it. The key to the concept of "Do what you hate like you love it—until you *do* love it" is to *focus* on what you *do want* rather than trying to *avoid* what you *don't want.*

What you give attention to grows. This means that if you give your attention to an activity you want to eliminate, that activity—be it physical or mental—unfortunately grows in focus, in size, and in importance. Giving it attention turns it into a cultivated habit. Program your thoughtlife with the success you want to create, and that is what will be embedded into the very fabric of your being. Water your flowers, your herbs, your fruit trees, and your vegetable plants. Don't water the weeds.

DANCE WITH THE PLANET

As we near the end of *Qreative Evolution*, I want to support you with a few reminders, starting with your place in this world. Life on Earth is a gift. Dance with this planet. Engage with the Earth with your humanity. Activate your brain by walking, remembering, and other human functions that trigger the synaptic responses of your brain that keep it evolving. My thoughts immediately bring me back to the story I told in Chapter One, when Michaelanthony insisted that I stop and enjoy those morning glory flowers. We need to flow with this living planet Earth. For so many centuries, we've engaged with this planet, tilling the soil, enjoying the warmth of the sun and the tickle of a gentle breeze on our faces, feeling the ground under our feet as we walked from one place to another. If you find yourself stuck or you can't see what you should be doing, do what our ancestors did: Move your body, go outside, take a walk, go swimming, or get in the shower so you can feel water on your skin. You can also go somewhere new that allows you to experience things in a new way. An unfamiliar environment gives you a fresh perspective. This last choice works for me. Whenever I begin to work on a creative project, I leave my studio so I can expose myself to new sights, sounds, and ideas.

Do not forget the physical human functions and processes that we have used throughout time to create and grow as a species. Here are some processes that not only built up humanity, but are necessary to help our bodies and brains grow:

- Crawling helps a baby's corpus callosum to develop so their brain's hemispheres can communicate.
- Handwriting activates the brain's frontal lobe.
- Memorization forms synapses between the brain's neurons.
- Reading helps memory, focus, and communication skills.
- Calculating improves cognitive skills and memory.
- Making food by hand honors cultural traditions.

- Socializing with others improves interpersonal skills, empathy, and confidence.

Resist relying on technology for everything. Give your brain and body an opportunity to grow and stay healthy by letting them do the living they were meant to do. As you purposefully create your life, participate in the fullness of creativity. Keep a record of your progress in your journalnotebook. That is additional fuel for your journey. Remember, you never "land." You are always in flight, progressing on your path.

Creativity is not always practical, efficient, economical, easy, or secure. It is often frightening, inconvenient, difficult, confusing, and arduous—at least momentarily—to break free and do something you've never done before. This is all as it should be, however, because the assignments that appear for you as you engage with your creativity are assignments that are vital to creating your life.

The most valuable message in this book is that you are in charge of creating your life. It doesn't matter how old you are when you wake up to this truth. It doesn't matter where you are, or what you do for work, or whether or not you are clear about your purpose in life. *You* are the artist creating your life regardless of what your life looks like at this moment, or what you do or don't know, or who surrounds you. When people hear me say that they are the creators of their own lives, they often ask, "What if I don't have support around me, or if I didn't grow up with a supportive parent or teacher to guide me?"

The answer is strikingly simple: *Just start from where you are right now.* You have this book. That is one source of support.

Whenever you discover your purpose, and at whatever level of your talent or expertise, you are exactly where you need to be. Your creativity is like a seed. It will grow when you plant it. Which is right now. You don't have to wait until you are "ready" to begin fulfilling your purpose in life. The "ready" is built into wherever you start. Everything you have gone through, even the hardships, have meaning and purpose. They have made you ready.

Nothing you've gone through is wasted. All of your experiences—the joys, the heartbreaks, the gains, the losses—have formed you into the person you are right now and can be used to help you discover your life's purpose. The fact that you are taking the time to read this book is a sign that you are ready to launch into the life you were meant to live. The next step is to embrace your unique and individual course in life and launch, right now, from wherever you are.

Life, itself, is the single greatest gift of all. A gift that is intimately individual to each person it is given to.

"What are the two most important days in your life? The day you are born and the day you find out why."
—MARK TWAIN

You were born with a purpose. We all were. And the great assignment of our lives is not to decide what our purpose is but to *discover* it. Enjoy this ride and embrace it with all that you are. May you discover your own way. By making *Qreative Evolution* a member of your "Library of Friends," you will discover the structure and encouragement to embrace your own life, calling, and purpose. May this book become one of your "friends" so we can continue this journey together.

Now . . . let us continue to . . .
EVOLVE!

CHAPTER SIX GUIDED SELF-EDUCATION CHALLENGE: YOUR TRANSCENDENT CREATIVITY

You have reached the end of the last chapter. Congratulations! It is now time to take massive action, which is why I close this final chapter not with an inquiry, but with a series of life-launching challenges. These are exercises designed to break you free from the rote thinking and mundane activities that might be cloaking your purpose and lulling you into a life spent on autopilot. This is a positive, powerful set of assignments designed to encourage your *Qreative Evolution*:

1. Sidewalk affirmations: Get sidewalk chalk in your choice of color, and then choose seven of your favorite life-affirming quotes. On a stretch of sidewalk where it is legal and safe, use your chalk to write one of these quotes. Take ten steps forward, and then write the second quote. Take ten steps forward again, and then write the third quote, and so on, until you've written all seven quotes on the ground. This assignment reveals what you've learned. And, if even one of your shared quotes catches the eye of someone in need of learning it, you will have awakened the part of them they need to grow.

2. Portrait of yourself: Using poster board, cardboard, or some other material, you will make a two-foot square "self-portrait" collage. Collect photos, pictures from magazines, clippings of inspirational quotes, and anything else that appeals to you. Choose images as colorful as necessary to reflect who you were as a child. Glue them to your poster board and hang the finished collage where you'll see it often. This is a graphic

self-portrait—of you!—that can provide meaning and clarity to how you view yourself.

3. Affirmation to the world: Create the most beautiful, encouraging, and inspiring message you can. Write it as an affirmation to help others feel a sense of hope and excitement about their futures. Design a flier with your affirmation. Make it as eye-catching as you can. Print a hundred of them. Pick a safe place to hand them out to as many people as will accept them. The very act of creating your "Affirmation to the World" will give you the opportunity to write something for someone else. It tends to be easier to give advice to others because of the level of detachment that exists. For this assignment, you will be focused on others rather than yourself. This objectivity makes it easy to consider someone else and how you might encourage them. After this, you can look back at your affirmation and see how it applies to your own life.

4. Theatrical self-movie poster: Think about what you'd like your life to be like after you fulfill your purpose. If this life were a movie, what would its theatrical poster look like? Create *that* poster. Designing a poster that celebrates your best life will help you visualize the life outcomes you desire. Use a title like, "The Naysayers Don't Get a Vote!" Then take a picture of yourself in a dynamic, powerful, and heroic pose with a subtitle that features your favorite quote in connection to your title and life. This should be a movie poster to top all movie posters! Once you finish it, display it where you will see it often. This idea came from my friend Ellie, who

I mentioned when I talked about my tribe. She actually made a movie poster like this with that exact title while she still lived in Jerusalem. From reading Ellie's story, you know she created her perfect life.

5. Creative discipline volunteer: Think about your gifts. How and where—right now—can you use them to help people? Volunteer to help one person, a group of people, or a cause, using one or more of your gifts. Give manicures at a nursing home, read stories at a library, teach children in an after-school program to draw, take a homemade meal to a lonely neighbor, play piano at church—use your gifts in some way to help others. Be creative and generous. This will infuse your gifts and talents with even more meaning and purpose. Every time I do this it brings me to greater heights as well as enhances my gratitude toward those who have helped me.

6. Dream company contact: Contact the company you would most like to work for and get their submission guidelines for employment. Take the first steps in preparing yourself to apply for a job with this company. The preparation stage may take a few or more months, but start now. Learn all you can about the company and its key staff members. This helped me get my dream job. When I am asked how I got to *Sesame Street*, I often tell them to do what I've shared with you here.

7. Catapult class: Find a course or certification program that would catapult you to a new and greater level in life. If it is pricey, begin to save up for it now. Take on a part-time job, if necessary, to earn the funds. Enroll in the course as soon as you can afford to. Part of

self-education is identifying skills that could help you grow, then finding outside education that will help you obtain those skills. Online courses are great, but there is nothing like the real-time experience of engaging with an instructor who loves the subject she is teaching. You'll also have the benefit of asking questions on the spot and getting immediate feedback and guidance and interacting with other students who are passionate about the course material.

8. Silence retreat: A retreat is a period of time spent focusing on yourself. What would be your ultimate vacation retreat? Identify this place and research travel requirements. Retreats are rarely free, so you may need to save up for this, but it is a worthy investment. Take this seriously because time spent away—especially focused on yourself—can give you a new perspective. Unplug from technology. Bring your journalnotebook and spend some evening or early morning time each day asking yourself life questions. The key is to design long and deep times of silence. The first time you do this might be challenging as it requires that you cultivate the practice of being able to focus on yourself. Any withdrawal symptoms will reveal just how far away from your ancient gift you've drifted.

9. Conquering your great life challenge: Identify the most challenging thing in your life. This challenge may involve your health, a relationship, your mindset, your mental health, a financial issue, or something else. Research the best professional you can find to help you. Begin the process of meeting this challenge, healing,

and gaining the freedom you need to finally create your true life. This action will let you see through what you once considered as flaws and accept them as the powerful assignments they truly are.

10. Unconditional love connection: Reach out to the person who has caused you the most pain. There could have been a rift between you caused by a disagreement, an argument, a split or some other unpleasant, negative incident. Or perhaps you each silently drifted off in separate directions, never to speak again. Explore what happened between you. Take full responsibility for the issue, ask them to forgive you, and apply unconditional love toward them (and toward yourself). This is a liberating achievement which I have done several times. Take it as far as you genuinely can. If needed, take some time to work up to it and get the help of a professional to help you prepare. This is a very sensitive assignment, so please use wisdom and discretion. Some relationships are meant to be permanently released. But if you know there is hope and room for mutual acceptance, please make an attempt to connect.

11. Your own test! No one else can challenge you more than you can. Following the increasing intensity of the above challenges, create your *own* assignment, one that will launch you far and above what the previous assignments can. Don't skimp on this. The challenge you present yourself with is your grand opportunity to see how seriously you take both yourself and your desire to truly create your life. Your test will catapult you toward greatness.

By this time you have seen the length, depth, width, and heights you can go with *Qreative Evolution*. Your vision and standards, your life itself, has been challenged in these pages. It is now time to show yourself how you will surpass even what you may have learned here.

How will you take everything I have shared with you and go further, to a level that only *you* can imagine?

Qreative Evolution is within your reach. Just look *within!*

ACKNOWLEDGMENTS

Throughout my entire life there have been many people who have helped and supported me. These are the individuals who have had the most direct impact on me and this book. The opportunity to thank these extremely special people in print is truly a gift.

Although this book is dedicated to my mother, Justa C. Mitchell, and my eighth-grade art teacher, Mrs. Charlotte Landau, I want to acknowledge them again, here. I will always take every opportunity to express my ever-increasing love and gratitude for these powerful, influential women. Mother and Mrs. Landau, your impact on me created a seismic shift that not only helped a younger me to evolve into the creative person I am today, but continues to (and always will) nurture me. Thank you for supporting me and my creativity.

My father, Reuben Henry Mitchell, whom we lost on April 21, 1993, couldn't understand how art could be a sustainable career. Dad, in your concern for me, you tried to steer me in another direction. After seeing me happy and successful while making a career of my creative passion, you became extremely proud of me for sticking to my dreams and achieving what you were unable to "see" until it manifested through me.

I constantly think about my sister, Juanita Stephens, whom we lost on October 26, 2008. Juanita, you said that you never had any goals until I told you I wanted to start an art school. You told me that all you ever aspired toward was to help me with it. With all your love and generous support, you helped me—and continue to help me. And to my sister, Margarita Vasquez, whom I wanted to emulate from the moment I saw you having fun with your paint-by-number set. Not aware of what a paint-by-number set was, I thought you were painting from memory and I was inspired by the fun you were having. You continue to inspire me with your beautiful custom-made cakes and the other creative ideas you always share with me. You make creativity fun.

Michaelanthony, my amazing son! You have always been, and still are, among my greatest teachers. From the time when you were a three-month-old playing repeat patterns on your little toy piano, up to your young manhood when you helped me learn how I could reverse my type 2 diabetes, you are among my greatest and wisest cheerleaders. I am indescribably grateful both *to* you and *for* you.

Stedroy Cleghorne, my very first best friend and fellow artist. We met in the fifth grade and quickly became each other's creative coaches. We elevated each other's artistic ability as we supported each other's creative desires, and looked out for each other. You're my favorite watercolor painter and it was you who inspired me to go back to this versatile medium in my own personal work.

Andree' Maitland, my dear friend, whom we lost on March 5, 2021. You meant the world to me and I will always make sure people know what an amazing artist, writer, and human being you were. The story about you in this book is among the most bittersweet, yet elevating, stories of my entire life.

Dorothy Wachtenheim Kopelman, thank you for believing in me and encouraging me when I became one of your seventh-grade students. You immediately saw the talent that I was unable to see, especially being such a nervous pupil in a brand-new school. You helped me focus on my creativity and you showcased my art wherever you could. It was you who encouraged me to apply to the High School of Art and Design. You believed I could make it in and I did.

Mark Rindner! You hired me on the first day I walked into your New York Comic Art Gallery (after I begged you to let me work there). You could pay me only with new comic books at first because you had only just opened. You wouldn't let me work for free, even though I was willing to work for nothing until you could afford to put me on salary. I could never have imagined that connecting with you—if only just to stop my fellow high school students from stealing your comic books, cutting matts, depositing the store's earnings, and buying your lunchtime Blimpie sandwiches (with provolone cheese)—would place me right where I needed to be to meet, then work for, my childhood idol, Neal Adams.

Neal Adams, my first boss as a professional artist, whom we lost on April 28, 2022. You stopped me from giving up on my art career. I had turned twenty and felt that I wasn't doing "well enough." I went to deliver my last art pages to you and let you know I was going to enlist in the army. You, however, encouraged me to attend art college. I followed your advice, and it changed my life. When I couldn't speak with my father about what I was going through, you were there, guiding me toward what my natural father wasn't able to believe I could achieve. I called you Papa Bear after that, and we remained friends for the rest of your life.

Royal Bruce Montgomery, whom we lost on July 5, 2018. Although you were my boss's boss, you took me directly under your wing, showing me a creative world beyond advertising art that allowed me to envision a creative career closer to my heart. It was your belief in my idea to celebrate Martin Luther King Jr. Day that led to my meeting Coretta Scott King.

James Mahon, my great Muppet guru, and dear friend. You were the one who opened the beautiful doors of the Muppet world to me and showed me how to grow, survive, and thrive within it.

Rachel Lunden-Carter, my dear, dear friend. You are responsible for the life-changing experiences I had with children with autism, which in turn led me to design the Julia Muppet for *Sesame Street*. You are more than a friend to me. I cherish your generosity, encouragement, support, and love.

Stephanie Plunkett, my leader at the Norman Rockwell Museum, who saw both my love of Norman Rockwell and my devotion to my favorite artists and turned this love into opportunities that led me to become a member of the Norman Rockwell Museum board of trustees. You accepted my own art into the museum's permanent collection, and you even invited me to write the foreword to *Norman Rockwell Drawings, 1911–1976* about Rockwell's drawings, my favorite part of his work.

Dolf Berle, my brother-friend, who observed me as you led our Rockwell Museum board functions and set me up as the artist-in-residence for Lindblad Expeditions when you were their CEO. Thank you. I had dreams of traveling to the Galapagos Islands, Singapore, and New Zealand, and you made them all possible. We remain great friends with many shared adventures awaiting us.

Trevor Crafts, you genius creator. You allowed me to be part of your (and your wife Ellen's) phenomenal team as you worked on the documentary, *Street Gang: How We Got to Sesame Street*. We became good friends as a result. I shared my proposal for this very book, *Qreative Evolution,* with you. You responded quickly with the most amazing encouragement, promising to share the manuscript with your agent to see if she could help me find an agent of my own. Your generosity goes against the stereotype of art being a dog-eat-dog world.

Amy Collins, my Godsend of an agent! After Trevor sent you my proposal, you responded in no time, stating that you wanted to be my agent. We've accomplished so much together and this very book is the result of your visionary wisdom and support of what is ultimately the foundation of the rest of my life's true purpose.

Stephanie Pedersen, my brilliant editor. After a couple of false starts with other editors, you immediately understood and embraced what my heart was attempting to put down on paper. My own writing needed the refinement to make it even more engaging, accessible, and clear. We became symbiotic from the start.

A very special thanks to Marilyn Kretzer, my visionary editor at Blackstone Publishing, who truly understood how to bring my message to the public. Thank you!

And to Blackstone Publishing for believing in me and my book. I could tell *Qreative Evolution* belonged with you from the moment we had our first meeting.

GLOSSARY

Throughout *Qreative Evolution*, I combine and create words to help draw attention to unusual concepts that can help you understand their meanings. I also use terms that you may know, but you'll see that I use them differently than they are currently used. To help you keep track of all these words, here is a quick glossary, organized by where they first appear in the book.

CHAPTER ONE

intimate: While this word is used today in a romantic sense, I use "intimate" for its older definition, which is a deep willingness to meet our creative selves in a way we have never seen ourselves before.

artlife: Another way to say "your unique life as a creative human."

launchpad: A starting point to help you build momentum as you progress.

CHAPTER TWO

thoughtlife: The life you live in your mind before you live it externally, in the physical world.

assignment: An opportunity to do something that will help you grow. This is my redefinition of what is considered a flaw.

CHAPTER THREE

journalnotebook: A companion where you record the details of your journey.

alarm words: Words that are warnings to identify negative thinking.

life words: Words that help you cultivate positive thinking and replace the warning words.

CHAPTER FOUR

replacement therapy: I believe the most effective way to eliminate bad habits is to replace them with good habits.

CHAPTER FIVE

tribe: Your special people; a group of supportive people whom you can count on.

mentor: These guides are here to educate you, help you think and keep you moving forward. Mentors are not confined to living individuals, nor do they have to be people you've met. They are individuals who speak directly to your life.

family: People who are committed to you, even if they don't share a blood connection with you.

relatives: People who share a blood connection with you. They may or may not be supportive.

RESOURCES

Throughout *Qreative Evolution*, I encourage you to find your own resources, whether they are books, films, music, artwork, places, or activities that challenge your preconceived notions and shift your paradigms. They should inspire you to go further and try more. They should provide you with a self-directed education in matters of creativity, humanity, and life.

Here, I share a few of my own favorite resources. Some of these are mentioned in the pages of *Qreative Evolution*, while others are not. All have helped me grow and evolve as an artist and as a person. They may do the same for you. However, do also commit to finding and compiling a list of your own personal resources. These will touch you in a deeply personal way that will accelerate your growth.

STUDIES

Askvik, E. O., van der Weel, F., & van der Meer, A. (2020). The Importance of Cursive Handwriting Over Typewriting for Learning in the Classroom: A High-Density EEG Study of 12-Year-Old Children and Young Adults. *Frontiers in Psychology, 11*. https://doi.org/10.3389/fpsyg.2020.01810.

Bersin, J. (2020, February 10). *New Research Shows "Heavy Learners" More Confident, Successful, and Happy at Work.* https://www.linkedin.com/pulse/want-happy-work-spend-time -learning-josh-bersin/.

Hill, P. L., Turiano, N. A., Mroczek, D. K., & Burrow, A. L. (2016). The value of a purposeful life: Sense of purpose predicts greater income and net worth. *Journal of Research in Personality, 65*, 38–42. https://doi.org/10.1016/j.jrp.2016.07.003.

Gazica, M. W., & Spector, P. E. (2015). A comparison of individuals with unanswered callings to those with no calling at all. *Journal of Vocational Behavior, 91*, 1–10. https://doi .org/10.1016/j.jvb.2015.08.008.

McLaughlin, B., Gotlieb, M. R., & Mills, D. J. (2022). Caught in a Dangerous World: Problematic News Consumption and Its Relationship to Mental and Physical Ill-Being. *Health Communication, 38*(12), 2687–2697. https://doi.org/10.108 0/10410236.2022.2106086.

Musich, S., Wang, S. S., Kraemer, S., Hawkins, K., & Wicker, E. (2018). Purpose in Life and Positive Health Outcomes Among Older Adults. *Population Health Management, 21*(2), 139–147. https://doi.org/10.1089/pop.2017.0063.

Scult, M. A., Knodt, A. R., Radtke, S. R., Brigidi, B. D., & Hariri, A. R. (2017). Prefrontal Executive Control Rescues Risk for Anxiety Associated with High Threat and Low Reward Brain Function. *Cerebral Cortex*, *29*(1), 70–76. https://doi .org/10.1093/cercor/bhx304.

"Sleep in America 2011: Sleep and technology," Sleep Education, accessed September 28, 2022, https://sleepeducation.org/sleep-america-2011-sleep-technology/.

Van Oyen Witvliet, C., Ludwig, T., & Laan, K. L. V. (2001). Granting Forgiveness or Harboring Grudges: Implications for Emotion, Physiology, and Health. *Psychological Science*, *12*(2), 117–123. https://doi.org/10.1111/1467-9280.00320.

BOOKS

Cameron, Julia, *The Artist's Way* (Tarcher, 1992)

Covey, Stephen, *First Things First* (Free Press, 1996)

Gatto, John Taylor, *A Different Kind of Teacher: Solving the Crisis of American Schooling* (Berkeley Hill Books, 2002)

Henri, Robert, *The Art Spirit* (Basic Books, 2007)

King, Jr., Martin Luther, *Strength to Love* (Cardinal Edition, Pocket Books, Inc., 1968)

King Jr., Martin Luther, *Stride Toward Freedom: The Montgomery Story* (HarperCollins Children's Books, 1987)

Jacobson, Simon, *Toward a Meaningful Life: The Wisdom of the Rebbe Menachem Mendel Schneerson* (new edition, William Morrow Paperbacks, 2004)

Keller, Gary, *The One Thing: The Surprisingly Simple Truth about Extraordinary Results* (Bard Press, 2013)

Nachmanovitch, Stephen, *Freeplay: Improvisation in Life and Art* (G. P. Putnam's Sons, 1991)

Peters, Thomas, *A Passion for Excellence: The Leadership Difference* (Grand Central Publishing, 1989)

Palmer, Parker, *Let Your Life Speak: Listening for the Voice of Vocation* (Jossey-Bass Publishing, 1999)

Palmer, Parker, *The Courage to Teach: Exploring the Inner Landscape of a Teacher's Life* (John Wiley & Sons, 1997)

Postman, Neil, *Technopoly: The Surrender of Culture to Technology* (Vintage, 1993)

Wurman, Richard Saul, *Information Anxiety* (Doubleday, 1989)

MUSEUMS

American Museum of Natural History

https://www.amnh.org/

The American Museum of Natural History is a New York City staple, beloved by children and adults alike. Its mission is "To discover, interpret, and disseminate—through scientific research and education—knowledge about human cultures, the natural world, and the universe." Located at 200 Central Park West, New York, NY 10024

Metropolitan Museum of Art

https://www.metmuseum.org/

The Metropolitan Museum of Art is another New York City favorite, featuring everything from ancient sculptures, clothing, art, and artifacts, to exhibits featuring the work of modern artists. According to its website, "The Met presents over five thousand years of art from around the world for everyone to experience and enjoy." Located at 1000 Fifth Avenue, New York, NY 10028

Museum of the Moving Image

https://movingimage.org/

The Museum of the Moving Image's mission is to advance the understanding, enjoyment, and appreciation of the art, history, technique, and technology of film, television, and digital media. In addition to exhibitions, film screenings, and live conversations with artists, filmmakers, scholars, media educators, and other industry professionals, the Museum of the Moving Image features a permanent Jim Henson exhibit, with five hundred artifacts, including forty-seven puppets. Located at 36-01 Thirty-Fifth Ave, Astoria, NY 11106

Norman Rockwell Museum

https://www.nrm.org

The Norman Rockwell Museum is dedicated to the work of artist Norman Rockwell, while also focusing on art appreciation and education "inspired by the legacy of Rockwell." Its mission, according to its website, is to "illuminate the power of American illustration art to reflect and shape society, and advances the enduring values of kindness, respect, and social equity portrayed by Norman Rockwell." Located at 9 Glendale Road, Stockbridge, MA 01262

Museum at the Society of Illustrators

https://societyillustrators.org/
The Society of Illustrators' mission is to promote the art of illustration, to appreciate its history and evolving nature through exhibitions, lectures, and education. The Museum at the Society of Illustrators features exhibits, lectures, classes, artist resources, an art shop, and a café. Located at 128 East Sixty-Third Street, New York, NY 10065

FILM

Bill Murray Stories: Life Lessons Learned from a Mythical Man (documentary) explores many of the urban legends surrounding comedian Bill Murray, a man known for his warm interactions with people.

Leonard Bernstein: Reaching for the Note (documentary) shows how powerful someone with a purpose is. The film chronicles the life of Leonard Bernstein, musician and conductor celebrated for expanding the audience of classical music more than anyone before him.

Light and Magic (documentary) is a six-part documentary chronicling how, in learning to create special effects for his movie *Star Wars*, George Lucas revolutionized the visual effects industry.

Listen Up! The Lives of Quincy Jones (documentary) offers a look into a musician, composer, arranger, and producer who changed the face of popular music.

My Octopus Teacher follows the unusual and yet very normal friendship between a filmmaker and an octopus he meets by chance while diving in a South African kelp forest.

The Beatles: Get Back (documentary) is a three-part documentary that invites viewers to experience the creative process of John, Paul, George, and Ringo as they write and record fourteen new songs to be performed at what would be their last live show as a group.

The Line King: The Al Hirschfeld Story (documentary) chronicles the incredible life—starting in childhood—of famed line artist Al Hirschfeld.

Won't You Be My Neighbor? (documentary) studies the inspirational success of *Mr. Roger's Neighborhood*, created by Presbyterian minister and former children's television executive, Fred McFeely Rogers.

CONTEMPORARY AND POPULAR MUSIC

"Better Days Ahead," by Norman Brown
"Brand New Day," by Sting
Can't Buy a Thrill (album), by Steely Dan

"Carry On," by Crosby, Stills, Nash & Young

Caverna Magica (album), by Andreas Vollenweider

"I Can't Make You Love Me," by Bonnie Raitt

Innervisions (album), by Stevie Wonder

"Killing Me Softly," by Roberta Flack

"Shower the People," by James Taylor

The Köln Concert (album), by Keith Jarrett

The Stranger (album), by Billy Joel

Thriller (album), by Michael Jackson

"Your Song," by Elton John

CLASSICAL MUSIC, OPERAS, AND MUSICALS

Carmen, by Georges Bizet

Hansel and Gretel, by Engelbert Humperdinck

Lord of the Dance, by Michael Flatley

My Fair Lady, by Alan Jay Lerner and Frederick Loewe

"Ode to Joy" (Symphony No. 9), by Ludwig van Beethoven

Sweeney Todd: The Demon Barber of Fleet Street, by Stephen
    Sondheim

Tommy, a rock opera by The Who

West Side Story, by Leonard Bernstein, Stephen Sondheim,
    and Jerome Robbins

"William Tell Overture" (William Tell), by Gioachino Rossini

WEBSITES AND ONLINE RESOURCES

Stan Winston School of Character Arts

https://www.stanwinstonschool.com/

The Stan Winston School of Character Arts offers online instruction from some of the world's leading names in character art.

MasterClass

https://www.masterclass.com/

MasterClass is one of the more well-known online lesson platforms. Choose a creative area, from cooking to oil painting to flower arranging, and take a course from a professional.

Chick Corea: Keyboard Workshop

https://www.youtube.com/watch?v=epFmSm26NGM

Chick Corea: Keyboard Workshop is an instructional video featuring the renowned jazz pianist, Chick Corea. His goal for these lessons was to remove the mystique surrounding the creation of music. The video was posted on Carlos Valenzuela's YouTube channel.

Academy Snippets

https://www.youtube.com/playlist?list=PLaQ1nfXt74Bnu-WKqNyaSHf8EZObcVCwte

The late Chick Corea's own "Academy Snippets," a playlist of instructional videos on his personal YouTube channel.

Ashes and Snow

https://gregorycolbert.com/ashes-and-snow/

Ashes and Snow is a meditative cinematic experience, featuring beautiful images and language. Created by artist Gregory Colbert, who sees cameras as musical instruments that can be played by the human eye. He uses his camera to, in his own words, explore "new narratives that help build a bridge across the artificial boundaries we have established between ourselves and other species."

Charlie Chaplin's final speech from *The Great Dictator*
https://www.youtube.com/watch?v=J7GY1Xg6X20
Charlie Chaplin's final speech from *The Great Dictator* is considered one of the most powerful speeches ever given. Chaplin wrote *The Great Dictator* to ridicule Hitler, a man who was born just four days after Chaplin himself. Chaplin, who was horrified at what the Nazi Party was doing, once said, "To me, the funniest thing in the world is to ridicule impostors. And it would be hard to find a bigger impostor than Hitler."

INDEX OF QUOTES

Asimov, Isaac. "How to Write 160 Books without Really Trying." In *Science Past, Science Future*. Doubleday, 1975.

Bradbury, Ray. Bradbury Still Believes in Heat of *Fahrenheit 451*. Interview by Misha Berson. *The Seattle Times*, March 12, 1993. https://archive.seattletimes.com/archive/?date=19930312&slug=1689996.

Cadini, Sabrina. "Be Yourself and the Right People Will Love You," February 26, 2018. https://sabrinacadini.com/2018/02/26/be-yourself-people-will-love-you/.

Lewis, Jerry. "A Sitdown with Comedy Icon Jerry Lewis." Interview by Martin Scott. *PIX11 News*, 2005. https://www.youtube.com/watch?v=ujt0pnvx1jE.

Luther King Jr., Martin. "Facing the Challenge of a New Age." Article. Presented at the First Annual Institute on Nonviolence

and Social Change, December 3, 1956. https://cfc.sebts.edu
/faith-and-work/martin-luther-king-jr-taught-work/.

Regan, Ronald. "Remarks at Convocation Ceremonies at the
University of South Carolina in Columbia." Article. September
20, 1983. https://www.reaganlibrary.gov/archives/speech
/remarks-convocation-ceremonies-university-south-carolina
-columbia.

ABOUT THE AUTHOR

Louis Henry Mitchell is an artist, illustrator, designer, sculptor, musician, creativity enthusiast, teacher, and author. Growing up, Louis dreamed of working at *Sesame Street*. As a result of fully committing to his creativity, Louis went on to become creative director of character design for *Sesame Street*, a position he currently holds. The lessons he learned on his path to *Sesame Street*—as well as in his life as a whole—became the inspiration for *Qreative Evolution*.

Louis was a child when his visionary mother observed how he was drawn to puppets (specifically the Muppets), artwork, music, and many other interests that she considered worthy of exploring with him. Their neighborhood of East Flatbush, Brooklyn, was increasingly challenging and many of Louis's friends were finding themselves in illegal situations or dealing with substance abuse. His mother, however, made their home a loving, comforting, creative world where Louis was encouraged to immerse himself in his artistic pursuits. From his mother, Louis learned to follow his heart rather than follow those who were distracted from their own potential.

Louis soon moved to a grander part of Brooklyn. It was in Park Slope that he raised his own son, Michaelanthony, who began his formal education at a Montessori School and progressed through the Cooper Union with a full scholarship. Louis shared with his son the creative life principles he had cultivated for himself under his mother's guidance. Watching his son—and others—utilize these creative teachings inspired Louis to develop and hone his creativity "curriculum," so it could be shared more broadly.

Learning from others is a key element of a creative life. One of the most influential artists of Louis's life is Norman Rockwell, whose museum invited Louis to join their board of trustees. This position has afforded Louis opportunities to give lectures, as well as interviews. Louis was also able to write a blog and several plaques that accompany some of his favorite Rockwell paintings. As part of his work with the museum, Louis was asked to pen the foreword to the book, *Norman Rockwell Drawings, 1911–1976* published by Abbeville Press.

As Louis travels the world sharing his *Qreative Evolution* curriculum, he continues to help people discover and use their creative powers. As part of his commitment to creativity and creativity education, Louis is currently developing *The Qreative Evolution* podcast. He is also establishing a unique art school. Both are built around *Qreative Evolution*, which is at the heart of his life's purpose. *Qreative Evolution* is a vehicle to share Louis's unique insights and his love and enthusiasm for life.

Find Louis online at:
https://www.facebook.com/louishmitchell
https://www.linkedin.com/in/louis-henry-mitchell-a087a26/